Contents

Introduction
by Craig Beevers

One of the most popular games on our colourful little planet. Most have heard of it, many have played it, and few master it. Scrabble™ is everywhere, whether it be played over a kitchen table, on the latest mobile gadget, or part of a national curriculum.

Scrabble is the toughest all-round game I have ever encountered. There are so many dimensions to it that other games seem linear and boring in comparison. It requires knowledge, an abundance of skill, strategy, risk and reward, luck, and a strong temperament. It is a complete test and a game I'm glad to be associated with. I became World Scrabble Champion in 2014 and I'm immensely proud of being etched in the game's history.

When first playing Scrabble I never really considered just how enriching it is. The words played showcase culture worldwide. A regular player will use the names of Greek letters, currency from every continent, a surprising wealth of old Scottish dialect words, lots of helpful **Q**-without-**U** words from Arabic, and a whole host of other weird and wonderful snippets of everything you can think of or has ever been. Not to mention the enjoyment of playing the game and meeting hundreds of different people from all over the globe.

In this book, I want to discuss all of the aspects of the game, as well as explaining the thought processes for a number of real-life game positions. Whilst it generally takes years to develop the word knowledge required to become a top player, anyone can understand the steps that lead to playing a particular move. So I hope that everyone reading can develop an understanding for the game and learn to play like a World Champion.

About Me

One of my earliest memories of Scrabble™ is loading up the cassette on the ZX Sinclair Spectrum 48K and playing against the computer with its gaudy eight-colour display. Before long it would come up with a prompt asking me if I was sure about that word I'd just played. Because it couldn't hold all of the words in its puny memory, it politely enquired quite often. At five years old my vocabulary was a bit shaky but I used to give myself the benefit of the doubt. If it wasn't a word it should be anyway, right?

That was back in 1986. According to my partner Karen I still spend too much time on the computer. The instruments may have evolved, but I still love my games. Having spent a lot of my youth with pith-helmeted sabremen, blue hedgehogs, and dark elves whizzing across the screen, I eventually graduated to more cerebral distractions. I got attached to the internet at college and university before wandering to my first Scrabble Club in 2003.

In truth I had been hooked by word games for a while, playing all sorts of them on the web. Scrabble was just the best one. I played my first tournament later that year and made it my goal to win a local one-day event, then a weekend tourney, and so on. *Countdown* (a words and numbers TV show in the UK) came along four years later. I took time out from Scrabble to concentrate on it and was fortunate enough to win the series.

Recently I've become increasingly involved with Scrabble associations, their websites, and running or organizing tournaments. I particularly enjoy being part of big events, even when I'm not playing. It also feels good contributing to such a wonderful community.

More personally I'm a mathematical, scientific sort of guy. I like my technology, but I also like to be outdoors and travel. I enjoy characterful villages and towns over big bustling cities. I grew up in Norton, near Stockton-on-Tees in the northeast of England, with a stint at university in Sheffield. In 2014 I moved to Guisborough, a lovely little town on the outskirts of the North York Moors with my partner Karen and three soppy little dogs, Molly, Benny, and Charlie.

My World

The journey really began when I reached my late teens. I had played Scrabble™ once in a while during childhood, but it couldn't compete with joystick-waggling on the ZX Sinclair Spectrum, button-bashing on the Sega Mega Drive, and later those countless hours juggling virtual memory in DOS, occasionally interrupted by playing the computer game I was trying to get working. By the late 90s, the internet was starting to take off, and that's when I got into word games.

Dial-up modems were the order of the day. I can still remember the high-pitched tone it generated on attempting to connect to the web, then me holding my breath on whether the attempt was successful or not. I loved playing games online. It certainly wasn't for the faint-hearted, but it never really bothered me. I spent many an hour chatting, playing, and arguing with Americans. I felt those across the Atlantic needed to be enlightened about cricket and rugby – much better than that baseball and gridiron malarkey. After racking up hundreds of pounds in phone bills, I went to university in Sheffield and discovered the joys of computer rooms with what was then super-fast internet. I moved from playing a range of games, particularly the card game Spades, to almost exclusively playing quick word games. I mostly played a clone of Scrabble, which had more tiles, a different board, and a love of dishing out **C**s, **I**s, and **G**s, which were all worth a measly one point. You also had to place each letter by hand. It was an adrenalin rush to beat people with seconds remaining at the end.

One thing that hasn't changed unfortunately was the level of cheating going on over the internet. It was mostly what's called "anagramming": putting a set of letters into a word-finder and playing what comes up. The quick games just made even more obvious the disparity between the obscure finds and the bad moves. Some even went further, having macros to place tiles almost instantly and programs (or bots) that played the game for them. It was a free-for-all. From the chaos emerged a number of players who have gone on to win big titles in the World of Scrabble.

Towards the end of my three-year spell at university I made the decision to look for a Scrabble Club. Being an exceptionally lazy individual, I was fortunate that all the details of a local club were on a website, only one of a handful that were. I'm not sure I'd have pursued it if I'd had to chase up the info. I always wonder how many people there are who would love the club and tournament scene but don't realize what is out there.

One of the issues of playing online was the difference in the dictionary, or word list as it's also known. The games I'd enjoyed over the internet used an old American word list. The international word list (Collins *Official Scrabble Words*) is made up of the American one, plus UK sources. I had a good knowledge of the most useful American words, but all the British-only words were new to me. Even more word games are available these days, with a variety of dictionaries in use, although the vast majority of words are common to all of them. So one cold dark night towards the end of winter, I ambled to Sheffield Psalter Scrabble Club, which met every week at a local pub. I didn't have a board but it wasn't a problem as there is always plenty of equipment to go round at clubs and tourneys. So I turned up with my pen and paper (the only essentials as both players need to keep score) with no idea what to expect. After a few timid hellos I sat down and played. There was a nice friendly atmosphere with a whole spectrum of people there from different backgrounds, from young students to pensioners. I won most games, but they were closely fought, competitive matches and I lost a fair few too. I fared reasonably well against everyone at the club except for one player, who beat me every time. In the UK, most Scrabble clubs and tournaments are overseen by the Association of British Scrabble Players (ABSP), who maintain a website, rules, tournament calendar and publish a magazine, amongst other things you'd expect from an association. The player who beat me each time, Lewis Mackay, was one of the top ranked players in the country.

One of the things most people don't realize is just how much skill is in Scrabble. At this club Lewis would beat the next best player nine times out of ten, if not more. The next best player would beat some other players nine times out of ten, and they in turn would beat the weakest player nine times out of ten. On a good night a dozen players would turn up but still this broad range of abilities existed. This is typical of most clubs.

After a few months a group of us from the club travelled to a charity tournament. I still remember flashes of it, such as the car journey passing Chesterfield's wonky spire. There are an awful lot of these charity events in the UK. They are not official in the sense of contributing to the national ranking system, but they're interesting little excursions, usually quite short, taking place in churches or similar venues and often raising money for a good cause. Whilst clubs and tourneys have a broad range of demographics collectively, certain events appeal to some more than others. So I arrived in what was something akin to a church hall. Raffles and cakes adorned the sides, with Scrabblers and Scrabble boards in the middle. I would be lying if I said there weren't a good number of light-grey perms about too. After an introduction, the first round of fixtures was read out aloud and pinned on the wall, accompanied by a fair bit of squinting.

I don't remember a great deal about the games, only that I had three of them. I won my first two matches by a comfortable margin. This gave me a high positive spread. *Spread* is what Scrabblers call the points difference. If you win a game 400–325 then you're said to have a spread of +75. It is accumulated over a competition, so if you win again by fifty then your overall spread is +125, lose and the spread is reduced and can become negative if you concede more points than you score. Wins are the first factor in determing a rank position. If two people have the same number of wins, then spread is the tie-breaker.

My third and final game was against a similarly young fellow called Chris. I was leading by 50–60 points and feeling reasonably confident when he tried **JEANED**. I had a feeling it was invalid, but as a relatively new player, you rarely feel certain either way about plausible words like that. So there's always some anticipation when a move is adjudicated. I challenged the word, and fortunately for me it wasn't allowed. Chris was ahead of his time, because **JEANED** was added to the word list a few years later.

That gave me a bit more breathing space and I went on to win comfortably. I then needed to see if other results went my way. If someone else on two wins had won big they would have overtaken me. Luckily that didn't happen, and I was quietly chuffed that I'd triumphed in my first ever tournament.

I say quietly because I have never known what to do with myself when I should be celebrating, although I'm not sure how youthful exuberance would have gone down on that occasion anyway.

So after a few more weeks at the club I kept on improving, but still getting beaten by Lewis. One of the beauties of Scrabble is that it has everything, luck included. On my final night at the club before returning home I did what Scrabblers describe as 'drawing the bag'. I picked everything against Lewis whilst he was crippled by awful letters. I'd defeated my nemesis and later sheepishly waved goodbye to everyone. I'd got the bug for Scrabble. I am a very competitive person, but also lazy, introverted, and passive. My academic studies had finished. But then they had never really got going. I was absolutely terrible at putting my head down and studying, so I relied on natural ability to get as far as I did. My skills growing up had all been about numbers, not words. Indeed, I had to redo my English Language qualification from school. (I thought I'd sneak that a few pages in and hope anyone reading has already bought this.)

Back home I'd been invited by Pauline Johnson to Cleveland Scrabble Club in Middlesbrough, a few miles from where I lived. Pauline had been the driving force behind the club since its inception in 1981 – the year I was born. In the early years the club played twice a week, playing High Score Scrabble. In the 80s this was the main method of play competitively – where wins and losses were irrelevant, only the aggregate of your scores mattered. This changed the game entirely, meaning wide open boards and lots of exchanging tiles until a big score came along.

Thankfully for me, Matchplay Scrabble took over soon after. Matchplay is the more technical name for what most of us would consider a 'normal' game of Scrabble, where the goal is simply to win. Cleveland Club is one of the biggest clubs in the UK and back then it had thirty members. It was more formal than Sheffield Psalter. Timers were used, all the fixtures for the night were organized in advance, and the games all counted towards an overall league or to the A/B/C divisions. Many of the members had been attending for over thirty years.

The best player at the club was undoubtedly Pete Finley. He had represented England in a number of World Scrabble Championships going back as far as the second event in 1993. He had a very posh board to show for his success. Pete and his wife Laura had met through competitive Scrabble more than a couple of decades earlier. I've since learned they were just one of dozens of couples who'd met through the scene. I always particularly enjoyed playing Pete. I loved the challenge. I was doing quite well. I was promoted into the A division and then soon after had my first 'official' tournament, which was organized by the club in the same venue.

This time, however, I struggled against a much stronger field, my racks didn't seem to flow, and I got bogged down in awkward, scrappy games. I won two games out of five, finishing eleventh out of sixteen. Since it was an official tournament I got a provisional rating of 135, but I knew I was a better player than that. The ratings ranged from fifty up through to the early 200s. Almost every national association has a rating and ranking system. Many players take a very keen interest in their rating and whether it goes up or down after a tournament. I loved my numbers, so I was among them.

Given my ample free time – I was unemployed and living at home with my parents – I got into studying words with a program called LeXpert, developed by M. G. Ravichandran. This mostly consisted of being presented with a jumbled rack on the computer. I then had to type in all the anagrams. Anything I missed was displayed. There's a bit more to it, because you try and learn words in a particular order, so you'd start out with the most useful first, and there are a number of methods to this.

It can be hard going when there are a lot of words coming up that you don't know, but initially it's rewarding because it significantly improves your anagramming skills, and you're learning words that will come up fairly often. Back then I wasn't really bothered about what the words actually meant, but there are always one or two outlandish words that come up and pique your interest.

The other program I used a fair bit was Maven, created by Brian Sheppard. Maven allowed you to analyse Scrabble positions. I found this particularly interesting, seeing how a computer evaluated the game. It also helped me to think about Scrabble; the value of keeping letters or sets of letters. And it showed me where I was making mistakes and improved my play on a more fundamental level, away from simply learning and then finding those words.

I felt like I was playing better each week. Later I played in my second tournament, where I won four out of five games and finished third. The year ended, and for the next – 2004 – I made it my goal to win a local event. I made a good start at the club, getting a new highest game. I'd won the match 660–260 with six bonuses against an opponent who'd beaten me by one point a few months earlier. It's a funny old game, and one that always keeps you grounded. I soon became Pete's bogey player. He was superior, but I kept beating him. More tournaments followed. I tried my first weekend event in Durham, organized by Pete and assisted by his wife Laura. It was a different experience to what I'd faced so far. Over 100 players in a university building, staying overnight, and seeing all those faces from further afield across two days. I did moderately well, but nothing to write home about.

Soon I was playing more and more events. I'd taken part in a national head-to-head knockout competition. I'd won my first match 4–0 but was eliminated soon after, losing 4–2 with a poor run of tiles. Looking back, it was easy to get carried away with drawing badly, obsessing over not getting any Ss or blanks. But ultimately you have to just do the best with what you've got and accept whatever happens. Soon after I had a great run of games in a local five-round event at Newcastle. I ended up winning all five matches and won the tournament. I had had my first win in only April, so it was a surprise and it only spurred me on to do more.

I had a great year. I won other nearby one-day tournaments in Peterlee and Middlesbrough. At the club I had completed all my overall league games. I was top, but Pete would overtake me if he won his last couple of games. Whilst I was sitting at a table elsewhere, he walked over to me and congratulated me. Laura of all people had just beaten him. I had my name engraved on the club shield and got to keep it until the same time next year.

Whilst for me the competitive scene was largely about pitting my wits against other people and striving for success, you do get a lot of different things out of it. Whatever level you're playing at, there is something to play for, with divisional structures in most competitions. Since Scrabble has so many elements, it has a wide range of benefits which aren't immediately obvious. Scrabble certainly developed my language skills, got me out in the world and seeing more of it. It helped me a lot socially.

I kept on playing and studying, winning the odd local tourney here and there. I enjoyed the occasional weekend event, usually pitting myself against a few of the top players from further afield. It was always a bit of a buzz to play a big name. I remember holding my own against 2005 World Champion Adam Logan before he pulled away towards the end of the game.

In late 2006 I found myself in contention to qualify for the World Championships. This was a really big deal for me. To make the England team I had to finish as one of the nine highest English players in the ratings at the end of the year. Unfortunately, in practice it meant players would get their rating up to a point they were happy with and then not play at all in the last three or four months of the year, so as to not risk a rating drop.

My last tournament of the year came along, a national team tournament involving England, Ireland, Scotland, and Wales. Because of so many players turning it down I got invited to the English side. I had a horrible tournament and missed out on the World Championships place. I could take the disappointment as I hadn't expected to make it, but how it happened – the fact that such an obviously flawed qualification procedure was in place and that people were gaming the system so blatantly – made me angry. It was one of very few bitter moments I've had with Scrabble.

Soon after I switched my attention to a different game: the UK words and numbers TV show *Countdown*. I had a break from Scrabble and tried to accustom myself to a completely different dictionary. I did my best to 'forget' the tens of thousands of obscure words which wouldn't be valid on *Countdown*. Unlearning words is much harder than learning them, because most Scrabblers are so reliant on instinct – just seeing words and not having to think about it any further. But I was now seeing words and having to work out whether they would be allowed or not. I was comfortable in front of the lights and cameras. Under such circumstances, with the pressure on, I felt in control and in the zone. This was important to me, as it's not something you can really learn. I did well in the main series, winning my eight games before coming back for the finals. After putting a lot of pressure on myself I ultimately won the series and felt extremely relieved. I also left a load of my shirts and goodies in the studio. Oops. It was a great experience and I feel proud to be associated with *Countdown*, a TV show with a long and illustrious history, one of the few things that everyone in the country is familar with. So I returned to Scrabble for 2008, amid lots of congratulations and handshakes. I felt like I was really gaining momentum and would soon be able to compete on level terms with anyone. My studying kicked in and I was on track to qualify for the World Championships held the following year. I had managed to scrape through to the National Scrabble Championship final, which was a best-of-five held in London and relayed to an audience in another room – a common setup in Scrabble.

My opponent was Allan Simmons, an Englishman living in the Scottish Borders. He'd been playing in competitions and writing about Scrabble longer than I'd been breathing. He was a familar face and we'd played a number of times before. After the odd bit of radio and some newspaper interviews, we were introduced to a few dozen spectators by TV presenter John Craven. The audience would be watching through a combination of close-circuit television, on-stage commentatry, and a giant Scrabble board covered in velcro.

After a couple of games the match was tied 1–1, with the first to three being the winner. The pivotal point came when Allan laid down **?NDIRON** for over seventy points. I hadn't heard what he'd declared the blank as, so I asked for clarification. **ANDIRON** and **ENDIRON** are both words meaning the same thing: a metal support for logs in a fireplace. I was holding a **Z** and the blank was one square below a triple letter score. He announced 'A' and I immediately threw down a cheap comeback with the **Z** making **ZA** onto the **A** for over sixty points. But I'd completely failed to notice that Allan had played an invalid word **NAIAS*** in the process of laying down his big move. It dawned on me soon after and I couldn't believe what I'd done.

I could have challenged his play off the board, although whatever I did he still would have got a similar score next turn because he had other options. But I would also have had the chance to counter with a big score of my own, depending on what tiles I'd have picked out. I went on to lose that game and the final 3–1. I had played moderately well, but a few holes in my word knowledge and that silly mistake had hindered my chances. I was disappointed and frustrated, but felt my chance would come again. Knowing I would be playing in the World Championships in Malaysia the following year helped keep me focused and positive. I resolved to do better, but the next year I got off to a terrible start in the National semi-finals. Played across fourteen rounds, two players out of sixty made it through to the final. I had lost two of my first three games and I had a mountain to climb. Things started to flow for me, and with one round to go, my fate was in my own hands. If I won I was in the final again.

I played another up-and-coming relative newcomer in Mikki Nicholson. She needed to beat me by at least 100 points to have a chance of qualifying. Mikki gambled a couple of times early on with dodgy words and lost. In a bit of an anticlimax I comfortably ran out a winner and found myself in the National final again.

This time I faced David Webb from Hertfordshire. He was not far from being a hometown favourite, living a commutable distance from London. It seemed to generate a bit more publicity and I found myself doing more interviews, in particular one surreal experience with a London radio station. I had been brought down earlier so I could take part in a live game played over the radio. There's nothing like playing a visual game on audial medium right? After a good few minutes of heated debate delivered in fluent cockney between a radio presenter and assorted eaterie staff next door, it was decided the contest should relocate into the back of the radio van. A few moves spanned a couple of hours and I eventually returned to my hotel to laze around and eat sausage rolls.

After a reasonable night's sleep in what loosely resembled a tenth floor caravan in the heart of London, I got on with the main event. David had been playing brilliantly all year and had risen to the top of British rankings. I anticipated a tough final. Fortunately for me, the tiles fell my way and I held the edge in the first game. I worried about getting caught up by a big **Z**-play from David, but ultimately I only had to avoid doing something stupid to go up 1–0. In the end, David not only couldn't get a big **Z** play, he couldn't play **Z** anywhere at all.

The next game followed and went comfortably in my favour whilst David struggled with poor racks. We had a break for lunch and did our bit of socializing and chatting on-stage. I got to trot out some of those tedious lines they must teach to sports stars in media training. Still, it really was anyone's game, as there are few absolutes in Scrabble. The third game followed a similar path to the second, and I triumphed 3–0. It was a harsh scoreline, as David couldn't really have done much more. It just went my way. I won £1,500, and after a bout of playing Word Soup on pub quiz machines with a friend and having no idea where the hell I was going, I got my train home and found a couple of rather nice camera lenses to spend my money on.

A matter of weeks later and the World Scrabble Championships (WSC) were upon me. It was held in Johor Bahru, Malaysia, just over the border from Singapore. I felt proud to be going over representing England as National Champion. This was the first time I'd ever left Great Britain and I'd never flown before. The twelve-hour flight over to Singapore wasn't too bad and gave me a chance to watch some films, but crossing the border was tiring. Two sets of customs and an insane amount of traffic. Motorbikes and scooters essentially filled every available space for miles in the lane next to me. As well as the Worlds, I had been invited to another tournament. The Causeway Challenge had been growing exponentially year on year, organized by the tireless Michael Tang. He had helped to organize the WSC in the same hotel as the Causeway, so the players had the two biggest international events almost back to back. Around forty different nations were involved, hundreds of different players, thousands of Scrabble games, and millions of points scored. The hotel where it all took place was part of a larger self-contained complex, with armed personnel outside the building guarding the only way in through a small car park. I had a wander about inside and out, but there wasn't a great deal to do. I'd managed to locate something which played a crucial role in my sustenance over the eleven days: a toaster, an orange plastic model aspiring to be a kitsch Bakelite number. I got by on a plateful of mini croissants at breakfast with toast, Maltesers and crisps during the day. I'm an incredibly fussy eater, and Malaysia being a mainly Muslim country, it cut down my options further, otherwise I'm sure there'd have been plenty of pork pies and sausage rolls to keep me going.

Scrabble or Scrabblers were pretty much everywhere you looked. Outside there were frequent thunder storms. I had a wander now and again just to try 90 per cent humidity. There were a few colourful birds and the odd butterfly to try and take photos of, but it was a pretty boring place once the novelty wore off, albeit incredibly cheap if you got away from the complex. I remember getting in two games of ten pin bowling for less than a pound, whilst the technology on the alley threw me back to the days of playing on the ZX Sinclair Spectrum.

After some glamorous ceremonies and free goodies (I've still got the shirt), 108 players from forty-one countries got shaking tile bags and the World Championships were under way. Twenty-four rounds were played over three days, then the top two went through to a best-of-five final. My goal was to try and finish in the top ten. The prizes started at tenth, which was of course a factor, but it was also an achievement to finish that high. I started off with a scrappy win before being drawn against two UK players... 8,000 miles to play Allan Simmons again and Phil Robertshaw from north west England! I narrowly lost both games, despite scoring 460 and 452.

I beat a player from Zambia to go in at the break 2–2. A couple of horrible games followed before I edged one back and drew great tiles in the final game of the day to finish on an even four wins and four losses, pretty much middle of the pack in fifty-fourth place. I got through my first day without having a disaster. I knew I hadn't been lucky and it felt like a damage-limitation exercise. I felt positive that things would get better.

After so many high-scoring open games, the next day started with an absolute stinker. You don't get many blocked boards at the top end of Scrabble, but this was one of them. I had the initiative with a small lead, but it evaporated as I couldn't capitalize on the openings that my opponent was forced into making. In the end I won 347–277 with my opponent losing forty points in time penalties. I followed with a routine win and defeat. Then I played two time runner-up Pakorn Nemitrmansuk from Thailand.

I was surprised to be playing Pakorn, because I expected him to be at the top of the field, which means he'd generally be playing other people at the top. It was exciting and tense, but I hadn't really been in the game. A few spectators crowded round and I nearly played a showy nine-letter word, **ITINERANT**, but managed to mangle the order of the vowels in my haste to avoid time penalties. Four straight-forward games followed, with me taking three of them, and I finished day two on 9–7 and up to thirty-second place.

I felt like I was still in with a shot of finishing in the top ten, but it was an outside chance and I'd have needed to win virtually every remaining game. Unfortunately, the next day started with a blowout in my opponent's favour. I kept plugging away, though, and managing to win one way or another. Meanwhile Pakorn had managed to win an amazing fourteen games in a row. I happened to be his fifth victim.

Suddenly I'd won six straight games and had made it up to ninth place. With one round to go I was drawn to play Andrew Fisher, a familiar name because he lived in England a number of years ago before emigrating to Australia. If I won I would get my top ten finish. Like the previous few games things seemed to flow my way. I had a good lead, and Andrew's bigger plays weren't scoring much whilst I was able to hit straight back.

I ran out a comfortable winner and watched the other results come in to see where I finished. Nigel Richards, the reigning World Champion, had finished top, Pakorn second. Both were on eighteen wins. I finished on sixteen wins and eight losses but had only moved up a single place to eighth. I was just happy to finish in the top ten though, with so many other big names. It also happened I was the highest finishing European player, which I was quietly proud about. After copious handshakes and a rushed ceremony, things got turned around for the final between Nigel and Pakorn the next day. I now had the opportunity to be on the other side of the showpiece clash, watching with the audience as two players battled it out over a best-of-five contest. I always enjoyed following games and tournaments online. A number of previous tournaments had included annotated games. These were games where helpers had written down racks and moves, which had then been put online and could be played through move by move.

Video cameras were set up so you could watch everything happen live. It was surprisingly dramatic, even things like tiles being placed one by one on the rack. Cheers as blanks and great letters appeared, groans as vowel after vowel or triplicate after duplicate were revealed. More noisy reactions as big scores went down, confused murmurs as moves we didn't see or expect got placed on the board. It was a great atmosphere and I loved it.

I won't go into too much detail about the first game, because it's covered in the playthroughs later in the book. So as you can imagine it was a humdinger. To stereotype a little bit, Nigel was the machine. He was Scrabbling perfection; he had his own style and would often baffle people with a move, only for it to then turn out to be the best play. Nigel did everything at a sedate pace. Pakorn was much more erratic. He once famously took seven minutes to decide where to place a word on his first turn. He was a very deep thinker. Frantic and fidgety as he was, he would often go right down to the last second on his clock, playing and picking tiles very quickly.

The second game was in complete contrast to the first. Pakorn was already 203 points up when Nigel's aura slipped a little. Richards had played **PIG** but had also made **IR*** in the process, an invalid word. Of course Nigel knew it didn't exist. It was a careless mistake and his just happened to be on the biggest stage. Later in the game Pakorn rubbed it in further by pretending to play **DINE** onto the bottom left triple word score, before saying it's not enough points and extending it to **PALUDINE** (an adjective meaning 'of the marshes') to hit two triple word scores for 167 points.

Another blowout followed, then game four came along. Pakorn, who had lost in two previous finals, led 2–1 and needed one more to take the title. The audience was on his side. The game flowed beautifully. **ADVENES**, **GRIFTERS**, **GENETRIX**, **DOYLEY**, **FREEHOLD**, and **BOHEMIAN**. But the board was getting closed down. Nigel led by fifty-four points and was looking good to force it into a deciding game. But there was still time for one more big move. Pakorn held **AABCNOT**, there was a floating **I** to play through, but it was obscured and any move would have to fit under **J** and **O**. Fortunately his eight-letter word slotted sweetly, making (**J**)**A** and (**O**)**N**. **BOTAN**(**I**)**CA** went down for ninety-four points.

ADVENES, advene, *verb, to add over and above*

GRIFTERS, grifter, *noun, swindler, one who makes money through deception or fraud*

GENETRIX, *noun, mother*

DOYLEY, *noun, same as* doily *or* doyly, *an ornamental napkin*

FREEHOLD, *noun, permanent tenure of land or property*

BOHEMIAN, *noun, an unconventional person, especially one involved in arts*

BOTANICA, *noun, a shop that sells herbs and magic charms*

Pakorn was now on the brink of becoming World Champion after twice being the bridesmaid. Nigel took a long time to try and find any way of winning. He made the best move, but it was futile. Pakorn only had to play any reasonable valid play. He declared the blank – '**S** as in Singapore'. Pakorn Nemitrmansuk from Thailand was 2009 World Scrabble Champion. He was overcome with emotion in the playing room and then later as he walked through to where all the spectators had been watching. Flashes everywhere, endless cheers and applause. It was amazing. It was not over though. After a lovely day spent in Jurong Bird Park, Zoo, and Night Safari across in Singapore, we had the Causeway Challenge to play in. Just five days and forty-five games of Scrabble to go. I got off to an indifferent start and felt more and more drained as the games ticked by. I was on the verge of another top ten finish and some prize money, but it was always just out of reach.

There was still the team aspect of it though. I was part of the second UK side. We'd managed to secure the top spot and received a rather nice gold medal each. We all got up on stage and raised a massive marble and glass trophy aloft. I narrowly avoided putting my back out and dropping the thing. Unfortunately it didn't quite fit in my hand luggage and we all left it to Lewis to take home.

After nearly two weeks away I returned home, sneaking my gold medal out now and then on the flight back. I hadn't been at the Olympics but it still felt pretty important to me, along with the top ten finish in the Worlds. I felt like I'd given a good account of myself in my first real foray on the international stage. In the years that followed I was increasingly involved with the ABSP and WESPA (the World English-Language Scrabble Players Association), the British and World bodies for Scrabble respectively, being part of committee discussion as well as designing and updating websites. I kept up with the playing side too, making the World Scrabble Championships again in 2011. This time it was held in Warsaw, Poland. It was generally around freezing the whole time. I can't say it was high up on my list of places to visit but it was pleasant enough and quite cheap.

My first game was a bit of a shocker. I was over 200 points behind and still trailing by well over 100 when in desperation I opened up a *nine-timer* (a move that links two triple word scores) – the only way I could score enough to win. I placed a **T** in the fifth position and then watched my opponent put down what I thought was **TRUDGE** and turned the board around, only to see he'd actually transposed two tiles and made (**T**)**RUGDE***. A somewhat costly mistake as I was sitting with ADEINOR. Off went his word and down went **DERA**(**T**)**ION** for 140 points. I still can't quite believe I won that game.

Over the three days I stayed up and around the business end of the table. There were thirty-four rounds in total, with the top two going through to the obligatory best-of-five final. I was lying at third at the start of day four, when I played Nigel Richards and drew tiles from heaven to win comfortably and go first overall. I then had a chance to put a bit of daylight between myself and the rest of the pack when I faced Andrew Fisher next up. Things were looking good when I was 150 points up, before Andrew hit me with a blank bonus. I was kind of expecting it because he'd been balancing for a few turns. But I was still in control, until he followed it up with **MOSSIES** (*mossie*, noun, the common sparrow) and (**L**)**UTEFISK** (noun, Scandinavian fish dish) to combine for a run of nearly 300 points in three moves.

I was still in with a shot at the end of that game, but couldn't find the vowels in the bag that I needed. After that things fell away from me. With three rounds to go, I needed to win all of the remaining matches to make the final. Finishing in the top ten wasn't even in my mind. My opponent started off with four consecutive bonuses and that was that. I just wanted to get out of there. I threw away any chance of winning in the last two games and ended up out of the prize money, down in eleventh place.

The final was between Nigel Richards and Andrew Fisher the next day. I still enjoyed watching it, particularly as it went down to a decider. Bonus words such as **ZENAIDAS**, **ACEROLA**, **GONDELAY**, **DAROGHAS**, **TOLARJEV**, and **OMNIFIED** were played. Richards ultimately went on to win 3–2 and became the first player to win multiple World Championships. The ceremony was met with much less emotion and exuberance than Pakorn's win, in keeping with Nigel's Zen-like persona. Everyone, though, appreciated that it was a great achievement, recognizing that Richards was the best player on the planet by a distance.

ZENAIDAS, zenaida, *noun, a wild dove*

ACEROLA, *noun, a West Indian shrub*

GONDELAY, *noun, gondolier*

DAROGHAS, darogha, *noun, (in India) manager*

TOLARJEV, tolar, *noun, monetary unit of Slovenia*

OMNIFIED, omnify, *verb, to make universal*

As more time passed, I got involved with running and organizing tournaments. It was a different experience, being behind a computer, typing results in, and generating fixtures whilst almost everyone else was busy playing. I've always found it interesting following tournament standings online, so being there and getting the results personally is kind of fun. Being a tournament director or referee, on the other hand, is extremely tedious. There are very few rulings to make. Scrabblers are a pretty well behaved bunch other than the odd grumble (although given the way the media dredged up controversy over the missing **G** tile at the 2011 World Championships you may think otherwise).

The global Scrabble scene had grown with a lot more events taking place. MSI (Mind Sports International) had taken on the role of organizing and running the World Championships for 2013. The format had changed a little bit, with the top four going through to the knockout stage instead of just the top two playing a final. With an Open tournament taking place alongside the invitation-only World Championships, there were an awful lot of Scrabblers about in Prague, Czech Republic. It was probably the best overall event I've ever been to. Lots going on, a charged yet friendly atmosphere, and comfortable surroundings.

I bobbed up and down the standings without ever being in the first four places. It was strange really, I should have been the best prepared I'd ever been. I had games I felt in control of towards the end that could have given me a great shot at making the finals, but I didn't feel up to it. I was struggling with mental tiredness and it was affecting my word knowledge. Which meant I was stressing myself out trying to work out whether a word I'd found was valid or not, and it felt like my intuition had gone, like I was almost word-blind, and I just didn't fancy being under the spotlight in that frame of mind. It was a relief once I was out of the running. I drew the bag to finish fifth and then relaxed and enjoyed the semis and final.

It again went down to the fifth game in the best-of-five final to decide the title. One unlikely move followed another. **ADEGMPU** went perfectly with a **Z** for **GA(Z)UMPED**. Then **BEJEWEL**. Then an outrageous play of **AUR(O)REAN** (adjective, relating to the dawn), with six overlaps (played words that overlap with other words) for ninety-eight points. Ultimately Nigel Richards ran away with the game and was crowned World Champion for a third time, beating Thailand's Komol Panyasoponlert 3–2.

So what happened in 2014? I did almost no word studying all year. I moved away to Guisborough with my partner Karen and three soppy mutts. I had played in one tournament since the 2013 World Championships, when the 2014 event took place in the ExCeL, London, organized by MSI. Being a complete cheapskate I booked coaches for £9 or so each way and stayed in a £12-a-night hostel.

Each morning I awoke miles from the venue, with an ever-growing pile of rucksack, carrier bags, and clothes near a window. I was still in cheapskate mode, and on the first day made it into a two hour walk to the ExCeL Arena by going the wrong way several times. Fortunately the tournament was running a lot later than I was and I had time to freshen up and compose myself.

This time the top eight players would go through to a knockout stage. I felt like I had a decent chance of achieving this, and then basically anything could happen. I got off to a great start, winning my first five games, four of them by a good margin. I lost out to a fellow Englishman before a nightmareish game at the end of the first day, losing by more than 200. I shouldn't complain, though, because I scored 728 against the very same opponent a few years earlier. The hammering pushed me down to twelth, but it was a reasonable start.

I won a couple of very tight games early the next day. My heart skipped a beat when I thought I'd miscalculated and, instead of winning by two, I was about to draw a game I'd picked great tiles in. But I went through the maths a third time and got the more favourable scoreline. I lost a game here and there, but won six out of eight for the day, and twelve overall. This left me in sixth place, and more or less where I needed to be.

By now I was getting into a routine of bacon butties (aka sandwiches) for breakfast, picking off sausage rolls during the day, and chicken fillets on the way back to the hostel. I'm sure there are better diets for keeping the brain going. I had plenty of support from home, lots of effervescent texts coming in regularly from Karen, being dead-batted by me.

As well as seeing how far up or down you've gone on the live scoreboard, players take a keen interest in how others are doing. You always want to see compatriots do well, but a lot of focus had also been on who was struggling. It never escapes anybody's attention for long when a top player is languishing down the table, and the best player in the world was having a bad tournament. Nigel Richards was well off the pace. He'd rallied slightly but was in twenty-ninth on only nine wins. Everyone was expecting him to still make the knockout stage; however, he was running out of games.

After some head scratching, I decided I'd need to win five games on the third day to make the top eight. I got off to a winning start, edging a high scoring game 487–479. A blowout next match put me three wins away. I'd crept up to third but it didn't really matter to me. Anywhere in the first eight positions was good enough. I won some more tight games and before I knew it I'd won the five games I'd needed. At this point, a few of us kind of wondered what would happen. I was hoping to sit out and rest up for the next day. But we all kept playing, and I tried my best to switch off a bit.

I got a nine-timer of **DYNAMITE** for 167 in the game that followed and eased to a comfortable win. A few people placed their attention firmly on how Nigel was doing and who looked like making the knockout stages. Richards had ominously clawed his way back to tenth place with two rounds to go, but still needed to win both remaining games to qualify. As I lost comfortably and quickly in my next match, my opponent and I had a look at how other games were going.

Brett Smitheram had beaten Nigel Richards; the three time and reigning World Champion was out. Even though we were all aware anything could happen in the knockout stages, it felt like the tournament had been broken wide open. I was among those quietly indulging in Schadenfreude. Later, after an extraordinary sequence, I won the last game by eight points after my opponent Dave Wiegand bonused to go 60–70 ahead and drew absolute tripe. I finished on nineteen wins and first place. The rest of the top eight emerged. Two Englishmen, two Americans, three Australians, and one Canadian were in the quarterfinals. As I finished top I played the eighth place finisher, Alastair Richards from Australia, in a best-of-three match. On one hand, I was trying to enjoy the fact that I'd finished top in such an amazing field, but I also realized that it would mean absolutely nothing the next day. I tried to look at it as having already won £250, and whatever will be will be. No-one from the UK had won the title for twenty-one years and nobody had come close for fifteen – before I took up the game.

I remembered how frustrating it was having no-one to root for when I followed big events from home, not just Scrabble, but sport generally. I grew up during a pretty lean period in the 90s: a few glimmers of hope in the football being cruelly ended by penalty shootouts; a cricket team that was awful year after year; an also-ran rugby team; barely winning a gold medal in the Olympics. Whilst I knew that maybe a few hundred or thousand people would be interested in what I was doing, it still mattered.

I watched England win the Rugby World Cup, and the Olympic medal count increasing every four years.

Cricket was my main sport of interest though. I've supported my local, county Durham, since their inception as a first class team. They'd gone from struggling at the bottom end of the table to winning a number of championships. I particularly remember the amazing 2005 Ashes, and Durham player Steve Harmison getting out Kasprowicz in the famous Edgbaston Test, when both teams were one blow from winning. It wasn't just the success or failure, it was how it inspired other people, the dignified way they went about their craft.

I had made peace with myself that I wasn't going to be playing at my best. I accepted that it isn't really about what you deserve. You play out a game of Scrabble. If you can do it well, you'll give yourself a better shot of winning, but there are no guarantees. When England beat Australia in the 2005 Ashes, it would be fair to say that Australia were by far the better team, and probably played better too. But none of that mattered when compared to the actual result. There are rankings for determining the best, but ultimately it is trophies that count. Sport is about producing a winner and a spectacle. I sat down for my quarterfinal match against Alastair. I was expecting to start the first game due to finishing higher in the main event. Instead we drew and I lost. Which pretty much summed up the game that followed. I was never in it. I was hit with **APIARIES**, **CRUBEEN**, **NEOTERIC**, **PTERION**, and **HARTALS**. The 166 point margin made it sound closer than it actually was. I resisted the urge to feel sorry for myself and resolved to win the next two games.

The next went my way. I started with **AADELTU** and quickly put down **ADULATE**. More big plays followed soon after. I was over 100 ahead, and every time Alastair got within striking distance I bonused straight back. I won comfortably 491–399 and got ready for the deciding game.

Once more I got off to a good start. Getting to a critical part of the game, ahead by seventy-five points with thirty tiles left in the bag, I was trying to shut the board down and clinch the game. I was going through a number of possible four-letter words I could play. Couldn't play **GLED**, because that would set up **OGLED** onto a triple lane. Didn't like the rack leave of **DREG**. Eventually settled on **REDD** and assumed my brain was playing tricks on me by quietly flagging up **AREDD**. It wasn't.

At this point I got very lucky. There were lots of **A**s to come and I'd just provided a great opportunity for my opponent to wipe out my lead in one big move. But he didn't have an **A**. In desperation he tried **BREDD*** which I challenged off. I had a bit more of a buffer, but was caught between whether to risk **AREDD** and lose a turn, or to try and obscure it. I did neither, but nothing materialized for Alastair to bring him back into the game. I'd made it to the semifinal.

APIARIES apiary, *noun, a place where bees are kept*
CRUBEEN *noun, a pig's trotter*
NEOTERIC *noun, a modern author*
PTERION *noun, a place where several skull bones meet. Plural pteria*
HARTALS hartal, *noun, a stoppage of work*
GLED *noun, a bird of prey*
REDD *verb, to put in order*
AREDD aread *verb, to declare*

Elsewhere the two other Aussies had lost, American Chris Lipe and Canadian and 2005 World Champion Adam Logan being the victors and meeting in the other semifinal. I was up against Dave Wiegand after he'd beaten Brett Smitheram 2–0. The semifinals were best-of-five, or first to win three.

I had played Dave a number of times elsewhere, not to mention the three matches earlier in the tournament. I got off to an inauspicious start by going second and challenging **FARCY** (a disease of horses), giving Wiegand an extra five points. With the aid of the blank, I soon got down bonuses of **(L)UNARIST** and **VITAMINS** to give me a decent lead. Eventually **MOTLIE(S)T** followed and I was in control. Not obscuring a cheap **X** play allowed Dave to catch up and put me under a bit of pressure, with the **Z** and blank unseen. It got a little bit edgy, but fortunately I drew the **Z** and that sealed the game.

One up, we both started the next game by exchanging. After a bit of a staircase pattern Wiegand hit me with **IN(G)LOBED** and **MIELIES**. The **E** in the latter gave me **TAILGAT(E)**, but crucially Dave could cash in on the hook to grab the initiative. I gambled by setting up a juicy **S** hook, but it backfired and I was left needing an improbable bonus. It didn't materialize. 1–1.

Not much to say about the third game. I couldn't do a great deal and quickly found myself 2–1 down and again needing to win the next couple of games to stay in the World Championships. The fourth game was nip and tuck throughout. I'd got ahead with **ERISTIC** and Dave edged ahead with **RELINES**. I was twelve points behind when I played **ORACLE**, keeping an **E** back. I drew **DFFST?** and sat waiting for what felt like an eternity to see what Wiegand would play. Would he mess up the easy **ST?FFED** bonus? I wracked my brain in the meantime trying to find an alternative elsewhere just in case. I pondered over **DESTAFF*** and **DAFF(I)EST**. Finally Dave played and my easy seven-letter word was left untouched. I put **ST?FFED** down, declared the blank as **A** (I don't know why, I'm well known for saying 'get stuffed'), and breathed a huge sigh of relief. Two all.

The decider didn't really get the game it deserved. I ran away with the game. It was anti-climactic, but I didn't care. I was in the final and had the rest of the day off. In the other semi, Adam Logan had come from 2–0 down to force a decider, but Chris Lipe blitzed him in the fifth game, opening up with **RECRUIT**, **REGENTAL**, **POLEWARD**, and **JUNK** to be 314 after four moves and eventually winning 562–443. So the final was set: USA's Chris Lipe versus Craig Beevers of England.

> **LUNARIST** *noun, a person who believes the moon influences weather*
> **INGLOBED** *verb, to enclose as in a globe*
> **MIELIES** mielie, *noun, an ear of maize*
> **ERISTIC** *noun, a person who engages in debate*
> **DAFFIEST** daffy, *adjective, another word for daft*
> **REGENTAL** *adjective, relating to regent, a ruler or administrator*
> **POLEWARD** *adjective, aimed at or towards a pole*

Lots of handshakes and wishes of good luck ensued, then I walked the three miles back to the hostel. All the time I'd been away my partner Karen had been texting me with messages of support. As the event progressed, I was on the online-streamed game more often, so a few friends and family got to watch me live. I can't begin to imagine how stressful that would be. I was grateful for all the remarks and attention, but also trying to keep level-headed. I tried not to let myself think about what it would mean to other people, as that would put on more pressure than just doing it for me. The next day I awoke to the sound of water dropping on the ground. It was raining and walking suddenly lost its appeal. I got all my best wetproof gear on and a change of clothes and ambled my way to the ExCeL. The weather never relented. I think my shoes were still soaking when I put them back on in the evening.

After a few bits and pieces Chris and I sat down at the smartboard – the Scrabble set with all the technology and cameras pointing at it. It would be our home for the next few hours. We were both wandering about in socks, slightly amazed at getting this far. I'd earlier made a comment about us being the two 'weakest' players of the eight quarterfinalists. In terms of rating I was the seventh best player and Lipe eighth. But it was all meaningless now. The first player to get three wins would be crowned World Champion. I won the draw to start and hoped that no more **ING-S** words would come up. A top player should really study those sorts of words specifically, so they know which ones take an **S** and which don't, but I felt like I didn't have a clue. I was mentally fatigued and just wanted easy stuff to show up. My first rack came **AAMNOO?** – aarrghh. My other weakness. MANOAO had been added only three years previously and I knew I was bad on the new words. I spent over five minutes trying to work out whether it was good or not. The game situation made it a much bigger error to play a phoney. So I chickened out and exchanged.

I got the bonus next turn, but more mistakes followed. I missed **AUX(I)NIC** for sixty-four. Unbeknownst to me, Chris had missed a few things too, but he moved ahead with **LY(R)ICIST** and I struggled with triple **I**s. Eventually my rack balanced out and I hastily played **(U)NRINSED** to go sixty-seven ahead. I kicked myself when it allowed Lipe to hit back immediately with **SINTERE(D)** onto the **D**, although in hindsight he would have got a bonus even if I'd played a more defensive option.

I was getting really low on time now. I knew my tile tracking was out but didn't know by how much. I played off my only two vowels, knowing there were still six more to come with four tiles in the bag and seven on Lipe's rack. I went eighteen points ahead and picked three tiles out. All consonants. I was sitting there with **BFLNSTT** with **AADEOOUQ** unseen. I thought for sure I'd blown it. He's bound to have **QU** and score. Even if he doesn't he can play out whilst I'm crippled with seven consonants.

Then **(Z)OOEA** went down. I'm still in this. I had less than a minute left. I knew QUA was out but wasn't sure what the other letter on Chris' rack was. I quickly played **B(E)LTS** through the **E** provided by **ZOOEA** and in the process blocked Lipe's outplay. His last tile was a **D**. I just assumed he would block my only winning play of **F(O)NT** making **(I)F**, but I was willing him to go somewhere else. He put **QUA** down elsewhere and my heart skipped as I thought he was going to extend it to **QUAR(E)** or **QUAT(E)**. I quickly threw **F(O)NT** down. Twenty-four and out. I was bewildered. I had won hadn't I? How did that happen? Why didn't my outplay get blocked? We confirmed scores, 403–389 in my favour.

> **MANOAO** *noun, a coniferous forest tree*
> **AUXINIC** *adjective, relating to auxin, any of various plant hormones*
> **SINTERED** *sinter, verb, to form lumps or masses by heating or pressure or both*
> **ZOOEA** *noun, the larval stage of crabs*
> **QUARE** *adjective, remarkable or strange*
> **QUATE** *noun, fortune, destiny*

I was still getting my head around the fact that I'd won the opening game when the next one kicked off with Chris' opening bonus of **BUNGLES**. I played safe again, not being 100 per cent sure of **FIRK** and being rewarded with a bonus of my own. I lost around eight minutes trying to work out if **BLOKARTS** was the new word that's allowed, or the old spelling (which had a **W** in) that got deleted. Eventually I played it and Lipe held the play before accepting it. I exhaled deeply and proceeded to draw my new tiles. I picked the second blank and got **OPERATIC** soon after.

Soon after I put down **PAYOUT**, knowing it was volatile but the right move, and created two big triple word lanes. Fortune favoured me as I drew the **Z** and got down **ZETA** for sixty-nine. Things were really going against Chris. He was over 100 down now and tried to open things up, but gave me one of the two *floaters* (letters through which you can play an eight-letter word) needed to go with **EEHQRSU**. I had been contemplating whether **QUEERISH** was good, but the **C** provided me with a nice safe **CHEQUERS** and the game was effectively over after seven moves each. I eventually won game two 524 to 419. I was now one game from being World Champion.

We had a break for food and I was able to think about the permutations, pondering how bad it would be to lose from this position, but knowing anyone could lose three games in a row. Better players than I had lost five or six consecutive games in the past. Even though I was out of the spotlight I felt tense and just wanted to fast forward to the end result and prize ceremony.

After what felt like an age, we got back to the Scrabble board and began the third game. I was going first and picked out my tiles. My brain was feeling laggy. **UPDRAGS** popped up in my head, but not straight away which generally makes me more likely to think I've made it up. Again I oscillated between going for it and thinking it wasn't a word. I chose poorly and opted for **PUG** instead. Chris immediately followed it with **JOLLIES**. I was playing catch up for the rest of the game, which flowed well for both of us. **GUENONS**, **SQUIZ**, **FELONIES**, **LIMBATE**, and **BIVALENT** for Lipe and **SHEDDERS**, **WRACK**, **OVEREYE**, and **UPTRAIN** for me. But I was kicking myself the whole time for passing up the chance to try the bonus first up. Chris had won 509–464 in a game lasting only nineteen moves. Sure enough I discovered **UPDRAGS** was good immediately after. I was left wondering if I'd blown my chance.

> **FIRK** verb, to strike with a whip
> **BLOKARTS** blokart noun, a single seat wheeled land vehicle with a sail
> **UPDRAGS** updrag, verb, to drag upward
> **GUENONS** guenon noun, a genus of monkeys having long hind limbs, tail and long hair surrounding the face
> **SQUIZ** noun, a look or glance, especially an inquisitive one
> **LIMBATE** adjective, having an edge or border of a different colour from the rest
> **OVEREYE** verb, to look out over
> **UPTRAIN** verb, to train up, to teach or educate

Chris started the next game off with **HYENA**, which mildly amused me as it is a nickname my sister has given me. Apparently I laugh like one, as well as being entertained by the downfall of others. I'll leave others to judge. Anyway the play gave me the floater I needed as I sat there with **NORSTUV**. After a bit of double checking I put down **V(E)NTROUS**. I immediately drew a blank, but a load of vowels to go with it. I got another low scoring bonus down though **GAIE(T)IES**, whilst Lipe kept scoring with thirties. Blank number two came out and this time I had more options.

Holding **DEIIOR?** I could score seventy-seven by playing a word starting from a **T** on the board. But it meant creating a massive hotspot. I didn't like any of my options, but I eventually settled for **DIORITE** and held my breath to see if I got hit by a big reply. Sure enough **X(E)NIC** went down, and despite starting with three consecutive bonuses I was only up by thirty-seven. I picked out two **U**s but had some scoring potential. A few more twenties and thirties followed for each of us before Chris hit me with **DIRECTE(R)** and my lead cut to just six points.

I spent a long time on the next turn knowing how crucial it was. I held the ugly **EEGLLLT**. It's one of those racks where you're desperate to play something tight but you can't really score either. I wanted to shut down the board but it wasn't possible to do it right away. I went for **GLEET** in the top right corner. It looked like an aggressive move but it turned tiles over, scored, and next move I knew I would be able to shut most of the board down. Sure enough, next turn I played **VI(L)LA** through the **L** I'd provided, killing an **-S** bonus lane which was always a big worry. I felt like a heavy favourite. Then I picked the **Q**.

I scoured the board looking for options whilst I waited for Lipe to play. He was only thirty-six behind, but I might have had to change the **Q** and waste a turn, or worse get stuck with it at the end. With fifteen tiles in the bag, I searched hard for ways of playing it off one, two, if not three moves ahead. Then I saw the **T** sitting next to the bottom centre triple word score. I could play **(T)ALAQ** there for forty-two!

I hoped desperately that Chris would go elsewhere. the **T** was a good scoring spot, so if he hit a good score there and took out my **Q** play I was in big trouble. I had no decent alternative. There were no **I**s or **U**s to come and none I could use on the board. Finally **LORN** went down and I got my forty-two points and shedded the **Q**. I had a buffer now, and only an unlikely bonus or a big mistake could take the title away from me.

> **VENTROUS** *adjective, adventurous*
> **GAIETIES** *noun, the state or condition of being merry, bright or lively*
> **DIORITE** *noun, a dark coarse-grained igneous plutonic rock*
> **XENIC** *adjective, denoting the presence of bacteria*
> **GLEET** *verb, to discharge pus or mucus from the urethra*
> **TALAQ** *noun, a form of divorce under Islamic law*

I looked for highly improbable nine- and ten-letter words, very awkward eight-letter words. I couldn't see anything and decided just to score and empty the bag. Now I just wanted Lipe to play something boring, not try a ridiculous bonus word that I'd have to wait a few seconds to challenge and wait for a big red cross to come up. He played **DENSE**. I played **BARFS**, making (**HYENA**)**S**. He then went out with **ET**. He had 414. It was 438 for me. I was World Scrabble Champion 2014.

Scrabble™ Terminology

Before we get into the meaty stuff, there are some terms to explain. Firstly, there's the notation for describing where moves are placed on the board uses a grid reference. On the board that follows the game started with **DOG**, placed at H7a. That means row H, column 7. The lowercase 'a' means the word is played across the board (horizontally), as opposed to down (vertically), which would be represented by a lowercase 'd'. Underneath **DOG** is **HONOUR**, which is described as a *parallel play* because it runs parallel to the word **DOG,** making **DO**, **ON**, and **GO**. **HONOUR** is played at I6a.

If we wanted to play the word **STRAW** from I12d, i.e. pluralizing **HONOUR** to make **HONOURS**, that would be described as a *hook*. The word **HONOUR** can also be said to have been hooked or to have taken an **S** hook. Occasionally the terms *front hook* or *back hook* are used.

The **S** in **HONOURS** is a back hook because it adds to the back. A front hook would be extending **GO** using an **E** to form **EGO**.

Also note that there are a few lettering notations with words. A bracketed letter or letters mean those that are already on the board. So if we wanted to extend **HONOUR** to **HONOURED** it would be written as **(HONOUR)ED**. Playing **DREW** through the **R** in **HONOUR** would be **D(R)EW**. Blank letters are represented as question marks in text, and when played as a letter they are printed in grey, for example the word **ST?RTED** with the blank as an **A**.

Tile tracking is commonly used in tournaments and often automated in computer games. If you were tile tracking by hand. you would start a game with a sheet of paper with a list of 100 tiles in a Scrabble set. As each tile is played on the board you cross it off the 100. The letters that aren't crossed off are often referred to as the *unplayed tiles*. There are also the tiles on your rack to consider. Taking these off as well leaves what are called the *unseen tiles*. Computer versions of Scrabble will typically display the unseen tiles.

Rack management is an umbrella term to cover the skills of an advanced player when they balance their tiles. This includes playing off duplicates, excess vowels, or consonants, and otherwise breaking up awkward combinations. So a player with good rack management will be more likely to preserve a playable or friendly set of tiles for the next turn.

Pre-endgame is considered to be the period when there are one to seven tiles in the bag. *Endgame* is when there are no tiles in the bag. *Late game* generally covers the period when there are less than 20 tiles in the bag and also includes the endgame and pre-endgame phases.

A *natural* or *natural bonus* is said to be one that does not use a blank. A bonus that doesn't play or fit on the board is described as *homeless*.

Countback refers to the tile values added and subtracted at the end of a game when one player has gone out – i.e. they have used all of their tiles and none are in the bag. In some parts of the world the values of the other player's remaining tiles are doubled and added to the player going out, but the standard practice used in the UK is when tile values are simply added to the player going out and subtracted from the player who has the tiles still on their rack.

Turnover relates to playing letters and picking up new ones. So a move with high turnover would simply use and draw more tiles than something with low turnover.

Playing Scrabble™

With the advance of technology, the game of Scrabble™ is more popular than ever and there are plenty of ways to play. The tournament and club scene is almost exclusively contested over a physical board, player versus player, mostly with twenty-five minutes apiece. Clubs are typically more social and relaxed, with many not bothering with timers.

Games on the computer or over the internet generally use what's called a void challenge system, whereby you can try as many times as you want to find a valid move and there's no penalty for attempting words you desperately wish were on the word list but somehow haven't quite made it in yet (we've all done it). Also, the software itself checks that the move is valid, as opposed to an opponent having the option to challenge a move. Other common rules are free challenge, where there is no penalty for challenging a valid move, five and ten point penalty challenges, and finally the double challenge, where challenging a valid move means a loss of turn, introducing an element of bluff into the game. This is played predominantly in North America.

However and wherever you play Scrabble, the core of the game is pretty much the same. But there are a few subtle differences which I'll address as they crop up later in the book.

What does change a lot is the experience. Virtually everyone interested in the game has played on the computer or had some casual games with friends and family. That covers tens of millions of people. But relatively few have tried or are even aware of the more social or competitive scene. Within that scene there are also a wide range of experiences.

I have played three-game affairs in church halls. I have played in pubs, a few events in schools and universities, masses of tourneys in hotels. Masters events, National Championships, World Championships. I even run a tournament in a train carriage overlooking the English equivalent of a mountain (a glorified molehill to the rest of the world). I've travelled up and down most of the UK, seen Spain, Malta, Austria, Poland, Las Vegas, Australia, and Malaysia with dozens of Scrabble friends. There are many more countries where competitions take place. Typically there are around forty nations represented in World Championships, and this will only grow.

Online play cannot really rival the tension, atmosphere, and prestige of playing in physical world events, as well as the social aspect of meeting like-minded Scrabblers face to face. Playing over the internet can be a frustrating experience, with cheating or accusations of cheating common. Having games against people you know should help reduce this problem. There are also a number of leagues if you prefer a more competitive and structured online environment. But there's no doubting the popularity of online play and it will always have its place as a more convenient and casual way to enjoy Scrabble.

I should also mention the Youth Scrabble scene, which culminates in the World Youth Championships held annually thanks to the amazing work of Karen Richards. Scrabble is a great learning tool and is part of the national curriculum in Thailand and Nigeria, helping to develop literacy and numeracy in a fun way.

Whether you're more interested in the social aspect of the game, the community, or finding a tournament to use some of your new-found understanding of the game on some unsuspecting opponents, the useful resources listed at the back of this book should help you find what you're looking for.

Overview

At the most simple level Scrabble is a points game. Score more than your opponent and you win. That's easy right? Well you will have more than one turn in a game. So building on that you need to think about the next turn. Most of the time there are a few unplayed letters that carry on to the next rack (your *rack leave*). This forms the basis of Scrabble – score and leave.

It is quite nice to simplify the equation by eliminating the rack leave and using all seven tiles at once, getting a fifty point bonus in the process. But for large parts of the game you will be trying to manage your rack leave whilst maximizing your score in the process. There is a balance between score and leave. Sacrifice score and you'll fall behind. Sacrifice leave and your rack will degenerate, eventually costing you a turn to exchange tiles and leaving you powerless to react to openings.

Scrabble is a word game, and naturally it helps to have as many weapons in your arsenal as possible. To get the most out of the game you need to know the two-letter words. These should become second nature after playing for a while. Being able to play parallel, making lots of other words in the process, is the bread and butter of Scrabble. A lot of the time your move should make multiple words.

It is also a great help to know a number of highly useful three-letter words, as well as other classics such as **Q**-without-**U** words and rack-balancing words with lots of vowels or no vowels at all. The two-letter and three-letter words are included in this book. If you want to learn lots of useful Scrabble words, or are just interested in words generally, then the resources section has a number of things to facilitate this. If you're really keen there's also the study topic.

One of the biggest misconceptions holding novice players back is worrying about opening up a particular square or trying to use a triple word score at the expense of score and leave. It is important to remember that there are usually a number of hotspots, and given the diagonal layout of the premium squares taking one hotspot often creates another. This often leads to the infamous staircase pattern, a common sight at Scrabble clubs. In the vast majority of situations the strategic value of a move is only worth the odd point either way. Always remember that your opponent can also benefit from an opening, not just you.

Another mistake made frequently is holding on to the pointy tiles, mainly **J**, **Q**, **X**, and **Z**, but also four- and five-point letters. What I often see is players sacrificing 10–20 points just to keep a big tile back. That is almost never the right option. It is important to get away from the idea of tiles you really like or dislike. Letters have a worth to your rack, which can be positive or negative, and you need to try to use them in the most efficient way you can.

Don't play to draw one particular word or letter. Occasionally it is the best move to play off a single tile (often the infamous **Q**, because there are lots of tiles that provide a big score and the **Q** is a big hindrance to it). I also often see players who have obviously drawn the blank tile and basically stop scoring altogether until they get a bonus, by which time they've sacrificed a ton of points needlessly. This is bad. Don't stop playing just because the blank is on your rack.

Tile Tracking

A crucial part of any close game, tile tracking is commonplace in tournaments and used by pretty much every top level player. If you've never played in a tournament or club game before but have enjoyed many a game on a computer or mobile device, then you may be familiar with automated tile tracking. Most Scrabble games online will either freely or at a cost display the unseen tiles – ones that are either on your opponent's rack or in the bag. When tracking by hand, a player keeps a running record of the unplayed tiles, then usually towards the end of the game writes these out separately, and only then crosses off the letters on their own rack. Crossing tiles off that are sitting on your rack would be problematic if you exchange, but it is safe to do it for letters placed on the board.

So why do players tile track? Well, the main purpose is to know exactly what your opponent has when the tile bag is empty. If it is done correctly, and that's sometimes a big 'if', this will give a Scrabbler valuable information in the endgame. It means you know exactly what your opponent has on their rack and can plan your moves accordingly. Tracking is also useful in the rest of the game, but becomes more important as tiles are put down and the unseen letters are skewed one way or another. To give a simple example, if there are thirty-five unseen tiles and only five are vowels then an otherwise indifferent **O** or **I** tile becomes something to be treasured. Although that's an obvious case, when spelt out it is easy to overlook if you're not keeping an eye on what is left. For those who want to track by hand, then one of the first considerations is the actual tile tracking sheet. I'm not going to tell you one layout is better than another. This is a personal choice, and I advise everyone to have a look at existing designs online and don't be afraid to tweak it to your own taste. Most people have the scoring and tile tracking on the same piece of paper. I spent most of my Scrabbling career doing it this way, but at the 2014 World Champions I kept score on an A5 pad and tile tracked on a separate and even smaller notepad.

However you track is fine as long as it works for you. I've seen A4 on clipboards with black background and white letters being filled in with a big black marker, I've seen tiny squiggles in a blank journal, and plenty of printed books filled in. It is very much an individual thing. Apart from size and integration, the other main point to consider is how you want the letters laid out. Do you want them purely in alphabetical order? Split vowels and consonants? Big letters, blanks and **S**s on their own?

It is also important to accept that everyone who's ever played the game has made mistakes tile tracking by hand. It can be very time consuming and distracting when you're not used to it. So keep going with it, you will get better and become more natural with practice. If you're using automated tracking then you can be certain it's accurate, but don't be afraid to play safe or double check if you're relying on your own handiwork. Count the tiles in the bag and ensure it all tallies correctly. Don't be lazy and end up kicking yourself after the game.

Thought Process

It may sound like overcomplication, but it is important to have an approach to playing each move, as well as when you're waiting for your opponent to play. Having a thought process will help make you play more efficiently, meaning small intangible benefits in your general play. It should also help to eliminate some silly errors from your game. On your opponent's turn (not applicable to untimed games on Facebook or similar):

- If playing on a physical board, make sure you've noted the score and added it up before drawing fresh tiles. This is standard practice in competitive games.

- If you're tile tracking by hand, cross off the letters you've just played.

- Be aware of how much time you and your opponent have left.

- Keep looking for moves. Don't just find one play you really like and twiddle your thumbs – have a Plan B ready if your opponent blocks your preferred option. Also consider that if your second choice is in the same area of the board that both plays may end up being unavailable when it comes to your turn. By looking further you may also find a superior play.

- Make a mental (or physical) note of hooks for later, or longer extensions that would score well.

- Anticipate – what letter would really help you out? Would particular floaters give you a bonus? By concentrating on positive outcomes it makes it more likely you could stumble upon an unrelated move which may have been there the whole time.

- If you're at least a few moves into the game then every so often you should have a quick look at the tile tracking, just to see if there's anything that sticks out – such as consonant, vowel or individual letter heaviness. Examine this more often and in greater detail as the game goes on.

- If it is getting into the late stages of a physical game and you're tile tracking by hand, then you should ensure the number of letters in the bag matches with how many you think there should be. You don't want to realize you've made a mistake on your time, particularly if your clock is running low. Panic is not conducive to playing good Scrabble.

- In the endgame phase, you should be spending a lot of the time anticipating what your opponent could play, how you can counter it and, if possible, work out the full sequence of moves.

When you're looking at moves:

- Ideally look at the highest-scoring spots first and work down from there.

- Try to find a bonus play before you even consider shorter plays and things like blocking. Almost everyone has lost games at some point by getting into a defensive mind-set when they had the opportunity to kill the game off with a bonus.

- Don't play or settle for the first big score you find.

- Look at the whole board; avoid focusing too much on one particular spot.

- Move your letters around, look at prefixes, suffixes and even just normal shorter words which may form unlikely compound words. This helps to keep your brain ticking over.

On your turn:

- Observe your opponent's move. If appropriate ensure it is valid or hold the play.

- If applicable, write the score and total down. Update tile tracking only if its necessary. Otherwise, do it on your opponent's time.

- If the board has changed, then check to see if you have any new, superior moves available.

- Decide on your play. Whilst missing a bonus with an otherwise average rack is a big mistake, not finding a bonus with a blank or two sitting on your rack isn't as disastrous. A blank will typically mean you get a bonus sooner rather than later anyway. Bear this in mind and try to use your time proportionally to the significance of that move.

- Factor in tile tracking as the game develops and use it to decide between similar strength moves, as well as to weigh up openings or hotspots on the board. Do you have the last tile for a particular hook? Lots of vowels to come? These could all have an impact on your choice. Tracking is particularly handy for when you have to exchange. Don't forget to factor in what's on your rack when you do this.

As well as the methodology of playing the game, there is also the psychological side to consider, for both you and your opponent. This is more emphasized in face-to-face play, but aspects still apply to playing online. Scrabble throws plenty of stress and absurdity at everyone. For the vast majority of people, keeping a level head will mean they play as well as they can. Realize that you're doing your best and that's all you can ask. Understand that there are no magical tile pixies out there conspiring against you. Accept that mistakes are made and Scrabble is not always fair and just. Avoid rushing and try to keep the focus on your next move.

I regularly hear about bogey players at tournaments. We all have opponents we seem to do particularly well against, or ones that we always appear to draw horrible tiles against. I personally don't believe in bogey players. Ultimately, if you play enough people a few times, you are going to have runs of good and bad luck that coincide with a specific opponent. The important thing is not to allow it to affect your game. Do not make it a self-fulfilling prophecy by expecting to be unlucky and playing poorly as a result.

The last thing to discuss is the approach to playing a much stronger, or much weaker player. I have been attending a club for over a decade, playing against a variety of opponents. There's an expectation that as the better player I will always have a bonus word or big score to hit them with as soon as a triple word score is opened. That is not the case. You can't play in fear of your opponent. Remember that a good player doesn't get luckier than you, and although they may manage their tiles better, they will draw as much rubbish as you do. Finally, don't expect an 'easy' opponent to provide an easy match. Scrabble is a game of luck and skill. Some of your hardest games will be against weaker opponents, and some of your easiest games will be against tough opponents. Whilst avoiding chocolate similes, you never know what you're going to get. Here's a quick example. Try to approach it methodically as I've described in this chapter.

The rack looks promising. Lets go through the process. Firstly, look for the bonus(es), broadly starting with the highest scoring lanes. In most situations you would have some time to think over this rack whilst you wait for an opponent to make their move, in this case **ENTITY**. So maybe you'd shuffle the letters around, look for -**ED**, -**ER** and -**IER** endings.

There are actually three seven letter words on the rack. **DOOMIER** (more depressed), **MOIDORE** (a former Portuguese gold coin), and **MOODIER**. Ideally, you would have the more familiar word readied if you're going through the permutations awaiting your turn. You would also maybe have a think about eights. There's only actually one possibility – **MOIDORE(S)**. – but no floating **S** tile has been provided.

Once **ENTITY** goes down, you can then look for places to slot the sevens down. Don't be afraid to look for multiple overlaps, there are an awful lot of twos, and it's surprising what can fit in. Hopefully you've spotted that **MOODIER** plays at I7a for a rather nice eighty-seven points; you would make a mental note of it. You should still also be looking for a four-timer or idealized triple word off the **N** (i.e. one with the **M** on the double letter). That's because they'd score slightly more. But as the difference is minor and the eighty-seven point placement has been found, you would not spend too long on trying to find something that's only going to be marginally better. Depending on the format you're playing, you would look for the high scoring eights first, but most players will have the sevens already in mind when play switched to their turn. Either way of doing it is fine as long as the highest potential scores have been looked at.

Rack Leave

Deep breaths, this is a big topic, and one that very few Scrabblers really grasp. There are many levels to rack leave, and each one adds to the sophistication. But whilst there are an enormous number of potential factors, none of them are complicated individually; you just have to try and consider all of the appropriate factors, and weigh them up accordingly.

The first level is to just look at each tile on its own individual merits. Blanks and **S**s are awesome, **Q**s, **U**s, **V**s, and **W**s are bad. Lots of other letters are in between. So good letters make the rack better, bad letters make the rack worse. Below represents the leave value of a tile purely on its own, starting with the poorest letters and finishing with the best.

> **Q V U W F O J B G I Y P A K X M H D E T L C N R Z S ?**

There are a few notes about this list of letters. Firstly, each consonant above does a little bit better due to consonant-vowel balance which I'll go into later. Secondly, each letter up to and including **X** is regarded as having a negative leave value based on computer evaluation of millions of Scrabble games, whilst having no tiles at all is neutral. But remember that all of this is purely an average, a starting point. It is generally a lot easier to find big scoring **X** moves if they are available, so for a lower-level Scrabbler, the **X** may be a good letter to keep, relatively speaking.

That list is handy to keep in mind, but of course Scrabblers rarely leave just one tile on their rack; it can be anything from none at all up to six. So as players get more sophisticated, they need to consider other factors. One of these is the consonant-vowel balance. The ideal balance is generally to have one more consonant than vowels. Every step away from this hurts your rack leave. I regularly see people underestimate just how bad it is to keep vowel heavy racks, particularly with regards to bonus friendly leaves, which frequently produce a rack of one-pointers with no scoring potential.

It is important to get a feel for just how good or bad rack leaves are. Most players will either not think too much about it, or they will have an intuition that is based purely on experience – and that is likely to be heavily flawed. Here are some examples that mimic the sort of choices you will make in a typical game of Scrabble. Which one would you choose?

1) Fifteen points and a rack leave of **?**
2) Thirty points and a rack leave of **B**

The blank is worth 25–30 points and would only be worth significantly less than that on a dead board at the end of the game. The **B** tile has a negative value, so generally speaking keeping the blank and sacrificing fifteen points is far superior here. How about this?

1) Twenty points and a rack leave of **ENR**
2) Thirty points and a rack leave of **INU**

Option 2 looks tempting, but in actuality keeping **ENR** back is worth a good few points and **INU** is worth taking a good few points away. So the first choice is worth on average three to four points more than the second. The **U** is a really bad letter and the vowel heaviness makes things worse, whereas **ENR** is a good balance of nice tiles. And another:

1) Twenty points and a rack leave of **AIT**
2) Twenty-five points and a rack leave of **AIO**

Only one letter different this time. But the difference in average rack leave is actually around ten points. So overall the first option is typically five points better. The leave of **AIT** is slightly below neutral, but swapping a third vowel out for a consonant has a big impact. This sort of differential is typical for leaves that are more vowel-heavy.

Okay one more, before we have a breather:

1) Twenty points and a rack leave of **AISU**
2) Twenty points and a rack leave of **AIQU**

Right, the **S** is a great tile and the **Q** is awful. Should be straightforward?

Well no, it isn't. The second rack leave of **AIQU** is seven points better on average than **AISU**. This is an example of synergy. I'm sure you know that the **Q** and **U** go well together. You should generally consider the **Q** and **U** combined as one single consonant. That is the best approximation because of how they are formed in words. After the **Q** and **U** you nearly always need a vowel to form a word. There are also a disproportionate number of vowelly **Q** words, so the leave of **AIQU** is actually worth around three to four points. The **Q** improves the rack leave of **AIU** by an astonishing seventeen points.

Synergy in essence means elements combining together to form something that it is greater than the sum of their constituent parts. **Q** and **U** are the best example of this. Individually they're horrible letters, but together they actually have a positive value to your rack. Other pairs of letters combine well too. It is important to distinguish between tiles that go together well just because they're both good letters and ones that have a synergy beyond their inherent values. Some other combos with synergy are **CH**, **CK**, **ER**, **LY**, and **NG**.

There is also what is termed negative synergy – sets that are actually worse than their singular values, for example **BF**, **BP**, **LN**, **UW**, and **VQ**. Looking at synergy more generally, you can see that hard consonants generally don't work well together, more so when you have not just two but three or four. This also raises the idea that rack leaves generally go beyond two tiles, so there will be lots of possible interactions, or combinations that work. So for instance **ING** has even better synergy than **NG**. And if we combine **BF** and **BP**, then **BFP** is even uglier – worth around negative fifteen points, whilst a sum of their individual leaves is minus seven.

Synergy on a smaller scale, with the exception of **QU**, is generally only worth a few points either way at most. But there's another bigger factor which concerns the interaction between letters on your rack and one that affects virtually every game anyone has ever played: duplicate tiles. Yes, we all get them. Not just doubles, but triplicates and worse. A second of any tile is almost always significantly worse than the first, the only exception being the **F**. So whilst a first blank would be worth in the region of twenty-eight points, a second is only worth about thirteen. A first **S** is worth eight to nine points but a second **S** is virtually neutral.

Why are duplicates bad? Well, they limit the combinations on the rack. If you have seven unique letters, you can arrange them in 5,040 ways. If you have two of the same letter, then halve that number. A triplicate means dividing again by three. If you have a second pair then halve yet again. This also generally hurts the chances of playing a bonus word. With the possibilities reduced, the number of words diminishes by an even bigger factor. As a general rule, a repeated letter is going to be worth around five or six points less than the original, and a triplicate eight or nine points less. A fourth repeat is a little worse still.

Here are some rack leaves, see if you can put them in order from best to worst:

1) **BMO**
2) **AEI**
3) **ENN**
4) **NRT**

These sorts of leaves would crop up fairly often. Lets go through them one by one. **BMO** has an ideal consonant-vowel balance, **B** and **O** are both pretty rubbish and **M** is neutral. So this is a poor leave, but only negative to the tune of two to three points in general. Number 2 is **AEI**, some reasonably nice letters and no duplicates, but the consonant-vowel balance is horrible (all vowels) and decimates the leave value, so this is comfortably the worst of the bunch. Onto **ENN**. This one is a bit trickier. The duplicate is bad, but remember that **E** and **N** are both good letters and there's an ideal consonant-vowel balance. So while the duplicate **N** does ruin things somewhat and makes it a negative leave to the tune of 1–2 points, it's still slightly better than **BMO**. Finally there's **NRT**. This is consonant-heavy, but with good synergy, which means you're ultimately one pleasant vowel away from a pretty strong rack leave. **NRT** is actually worth about three points sitting on your rack and is the best leave here.

Lets have another go. Rank these leaves from best to worst:

1) **AJS**
2) **EFS**
3) **RST**
4) **SXZ**

It's always nice to have an **S**. The main virtue of the **S** tile is that it is great for playing bonuses. Not only does it allow them to play most of the time by hooking existing words, and so has great strategical value, it is also great for constructing long words in the first place. More words contain the **S** than any other consonant.

But whilst the balance is nice, the **J** and **F** spoil things somewhat. **RST** is consonant-heavy, but it is a great bonus combination. **SXZ** provides a lot of ways to score; however, with the vowel shortage, they don't combine well and mean your options are restricted. So **RST** is the strongest leave by a few points, **EFS** and **SXZ** are about neck and neck, and another point or so behind is **AJS**.

You will notice I'm bringing up the likelihood of bonuses with respect to rack leaves. This is highly important for playing good Scrabble. It isn't just about how a few letters go together nicely and consistently churning out solid scores. Some parts of the game will be about managing a strong set of tiles with the expectation that you will more likely than not bonus on your next move. Even if you get a bit unlucky and draw some high-scoring tiles that mess things up, you will still have such good letters to fall back on that you'll often at least be able to get a good 40–50 points anyway.

One of the key factors in rack leave is volatility. As you keep more tiles, the randomness of what you draw from the bag has less influence on the goodness – or badness – of your rack. This is particularly important with respect to bonuses or what are called bonus-friendly leaves – ones that are very conducive to a bonus play next move. Unless the rack includes an **S** or blank, then any three or four tile leave is never going to be particularly strong, because it leaves so much to chance.

One of the strongest four-tile rack leaves is **ENRT**. This is worth on average twelve points. Now, the fifth letter you combine with it is crucial. It can completely cripple the bonus potential, or it can enhance it. It is a consonant-heavy leave, so a vowel would really help (although incidentally an **S** would boost the value of the leave by a further sixteen points). So a non-duplicate vowel is best, e.g. an **A** or an **I**. An **O** or an **E** also enhance the rack, but not by much. We'll go with an **I**, so **EINRT** is a rack leave now typically worth twenty points.

So a pretty average tile has improved things by eight points. We'll go one letter further. What would combine really well with our five-tile leave? We have **EINRT**. It is well balanced, so either a consonant or vowel are possibilities. **S** is still a brilliant tile as expected, this time boosting the leave by seventeen points. But there are two other tiles that go particularly well: the **A** and the **G**. In contrast, the **Q** would decrease the rack leave by over twenty-two points, so **EINQRT** is actually a negative leave – you're better off keeping no tiles at all than keeping **EINQRT**.

So **EINRT** + **A** is worth around twenty-nine points, **EINRT** + **G** about twenty-six, and **EINRT** + **Q** is worth minus three. What a difference one letter can make. It is crucial to understand the importance of bonus-friendly leaves, and as the volatility reduces how much more powerful a good, balanced combination of letters is. For most of the game, the chances of playing a bonus next move are significant odds against. Even the very best players will only average two to three bonuses a game. So you can imagine if your bonus chances increase from 25 per cent to 75 per cent, that means you're getting a fifty point bonus three times out of four instead of once in four. That improvement in odds means an extra twenty-five points on average, without taking into account the actual words played.

The blank makes things a little bit more complicated, because your odds of a big score are pretty good even if you simply hold a blank and draw six random tiles. So having a really nice bonus-friendly set of letters is a little less important. It's more about avoiding awkward combinations that will prevent you scoring or getting a bonus play down. Cashing the blank in will generally happen sooner rather than later.

Lets compare some more rack leaves:

1) **AENOR**
2) **AEILR**

Two similar sorts of racks, but one is around eight points better than the other. The second set is worth 11–12 points on your rack because the **L** is quite vowel-friendly and the letters all combine well. The **O** really kills the first leave, so it is only worth three to four points. You will often find that the **I** tile is much better for bonus-friendly racks than the **O**. If you swap the **O** for **I** and get **AEINR**, then it is virtually as good as **AEILR**. This sort of synergy is important when keeping somewhat vowelly racks, because without it you'll find yourself scoring poorly for numerous turns waiting for an ordinary rack to mature into a bonus.

1) **AGILN**
2) **AELNT**

Individually, the second rack is better. An **E** is better than an **I** and a **T** is better than a **G**, whilst the other letters are the same. What about collectively? Well, they're both pretty strong. Normally **L** and **N** don't go that well together, but the **G** and the **T** help things along. A big factor is the **ING**. It is quite hard to pick up intuitively, but **AGILN** is actually worth around nineteen points, which is very strong. Don't worry too much if you were way off on this one. That value is over five points more than **AELNT**, which is a nice leave, but just doesn't go together nearly as well.

Okay that's enough of the nice stuff. Here come the ugly rack leaves:

1) **AA**
2) **AIO**

This is often a choice to make in games: more vowels or suffer the duplicate and get a superior balance? Well, in this case the first option, involving the duplicate, is around three points better than **AIO**. It would become marginal if you were keeping a pair of **I**s or **O**s. A pair of **E**s is comfortably better than any three-vowel leave. Throwing **U**s into the equation makes things a lot worse of course.

1) **AANN**
2) **AAAN**

Two pairs against three of a kind. The latter would win in a card game, but what about in Scrabble? In almost every instance, having two pairs is better than a triplicate, or rather not as bad. Neither leave is catastrophically awful, because it should usually be quite easy to balance the rack next turn whilst still having plenty of words available, and there's still an outside chance of a bonus.

1) **BITW**
2) **FGLU**

So these are both quite clunky leaves, no duplicates so shouldn't be too disabling for the next move, but neither option is likely to yield a great score. This one mainly comes down to synergy, and the **-FUL** combination. **FGLU** is still a pretty bad set of letters, but at least it is better than the sum of the individual letters. **BITW** has no positive synergy. It's a just a rubbish assortment of tiles.

To summarize everything about rack leave so far: you have the letters individually, how good or bad each one is. Some add value, others are a hindrance and take it away. Then you have the idea of consonant-vowel balance: having one more consonant than vowel is ideal, and the more you get away from that, the more damaging it is. But there are a few adjustments to be aware of for letters which have particular properties, that combine particularly well with vowels or with other consonants. Then there's the letter **Y**, which is considered a consonant but often has the utility of a vowel.

Then there is synergy: how well tiles combine together, such as **QU** and common prefixes and suffixes. Then how a duplicate is almost never as good, or worse than just one of a letter. Finally, there's awareness of volatility: how many tiles are kept and how that impacts on bonus-friendly leaves.

These are not easy concepts for anyone, and I don't expect any player to get a good grasp without years of practice. The key is to get a solid understanding of the factors involved, and with those sound fundamentals in place, experience has something accurate to build upon.

The table that follows lists a range of rack leave values from minus twenty-five through to forty-one. Don't be intimidated. The principle remains to develop a feel and not worry about the actual numbers, which are there just to illustrate the significance.

Value	Rack Leave
-25	**AAEEU DFGPRR IOOU OOOQ UUUX**
-24	**AAAU AEEIU CDGTV GGPTW GTVV**
-23	**AAOO AEIOU AOOU CCTTT IUU**
-22	**AAIU BGRTV BUVW EOOU GOUU**
-21	**BCDGT BFGP IIIY QVW VVW**
-20	**ANNUU BFLNN CGMV IOUW RRRR UVV**

-19	EEOU EIOU FGOUV LMPQ OOO
-18	AAEO LLRTT LNNN OUVW UWW
-17	AEEU EEEI QV UU UVW
-16	ACGMV DDTT FIOPU GGG IOU
-15	AAEI GIOU IOO OOVW VV
-14	ABFOO AEEI AIU BGP EIOTU GIPV OOV QW
-13	EEU EOO FGIOU IJVW LLL NNTT
-12	AAERU AAI AALU EEE GLNTT WW WU
-11	AARU BPU FGOU GRTT II OVW
-10	AAE AEU AEIRU BGOU CEGMT CGP OO OU
-9	ABGIO AORU EEI GG IQ Q CDLL
-8	AA AEFV AU BB BP DLNRT EEET
-7	ABF AANN BCU CV EIVW GIW OTU
-6	AEI BMU EEW LLR NRR U
-5	ACEU AEGI CGO DD JMPU LMRT OWX W
-4	AENO CC DGO DIJOT EE EELNO FLU JO NU QS
-3	BDI EV J LNRT O RU
-2	AE AJ AMOP EF ETW LNR OP OX
-1	ADI AK BLR DO IJSU X
0	(an empty rack) AANR AEER DVVW? EENNR IT OSU
1	AEIN AENOP AIORT C GIR HT LY
2	AL CK EFLNO EM EORV GN IN MOOZ
3	CKY CEX EER ET ILN QU RT XZ
4	AELX AINOT AKLY DE DEIJN IOS Z
5	ACJK ATZ BS CHT EEINT EIKL EQU GS
6	AILN ART EINNT EORTX ER EZ
7	ABEL AELN AESV AINR CEKL EPR
8	ACHL CEH EEIRT EILR ENR GIN IS
9	AENT EIRRT ERZ HS GINT S
10	ACHT AES CENR EIRTT ERT QSU SST
11	AELR ACHLT AILQU AQTU EILPR EIRZ
12	ADEILT AERTT CEHT ENRT GILNT PRS
13	AERT AEIRT DENRU EIQTU ENORT GINR IRS
14	ACEKR AEIRZ ARS EIPS EILRT ESZ
15	ADRS AEQRU CEHR CEORT EIPRT
16	ACHRT ANES DEILNT EISZ ORSST Q?

17	AEILPR AEMRT CEIRT EGILN EST ORST
18	AEPRT AEST AGINZ EERS EIKLNT IRST
19	ACEHT AGILN ERS FOU? INST
20	ACERT AEILNT ARST EINRT EIRS NNP?
21	AERS DEHIRT EGINR ENST EPRSU J?
22	AEILRT AU? EORSTV ENOST ERSTT
23	AV? AEMNS EEINRT EIRSZ ENORS GILNS
24	ADEIRT DEILS EIMNS ERSTU X?
25	AGINS DERST EGILNT EOPRS GINRS MU?
26	AEIRSZ AENRS EILRS ERST EGINRT
27	AENST ACEHLT EF? EILST ERSTTU
28	AAERST AEINSZ AELRS ENRST ?
29	AGIMNS CEHRS EERST EORST AEINRT QU?
30	AEGINZ AEMPRS EILPRS E? NT?
31	ACEHNS AEMNRS CK? EIRST RT?
32	ACEKRS AEGNRS AERSTT EGINST EM?
33	ACENRS AGINRS AZ? EIMPRS ILT?
34	AECHRT AQU? CEHRST CEHIRS CH?
35	AEIRST CEIPRS ENORST ER? S?
36	ACELRS AENRST EGINRS ENT? EOPRST
37	ACEHST AELPRS AZE? EINRST GIN?
38	ACERST AELN? AENRST EHORST ERT?
39	AEHRST AEMRST EHIRST CEH? EIMR?
40	ACS? AEHR? AGIN? CDER? CHKO?
41	ACEHRS ADER? CES? CIMS? ??

There is an amazingly helpful tool online at *cross-tables.com* (the exact link is detailed in the resources section of this book) which helped to create what you've just seen over the past few pages. Humans (well, with the odd exception) cannot begin to memorize all the particular nuances with different rack leaves; nor could every possible combination of tiles be printed here. I highly recommend visiting the site and putting combinations of letters in. See for yourself how much a single tile can then improve or decimate the rack leave.

However, there is still more to this large topic. So far everything has been simplified somewhat with lots of quoted figures, which are merely an approximation or guideline. So if keeping back a set of tiles is said to be worth fifteen points, then that's an average value. It is a starting point. These numbers are given to illustrate the significance. There are two other factors that influence rack leave: the board situation and unseen tiles.

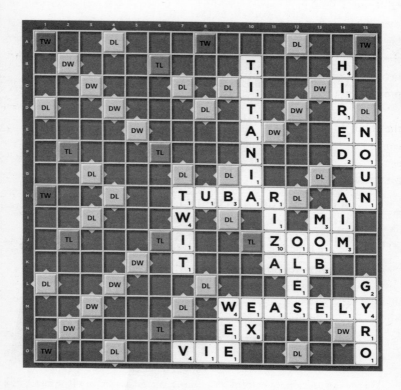

This is a fairly typical Scrabble board nearing the halfway stage. It is quite open, but nothing too outlandish otherwise. Imagine you're keeping **IQ** back. That's a pretty bad leave right? On average it is worth minus nine points. But that's a generalization. What would it be worth in this situation? There are two big spots for **QI** (noun, variant of *chi*, vital energy in Chinese medicine) regardless of anything else, scoring sixty-four and forty-four. Certain letters will improve that score a little bit more (such as **N** for **QIN**), and there's still an outside chance of a miracle draw that results in a bonus. So, to emphasize the point further, a leave of **IQ** here is actually positive and worth around 11–12 points. This was quite an extreme example, with a big spot open and a backup elsewhere, as well as having ready-made plays. It is quite common to have high-scoring cheap plays available for the *power tiles* (the high-scoring **J**, **Q**, **X**, and **Z** tiles) in games, so that part isn't unusual. Generally, though, there'll be much more risk or uncertainty attached. There may only be one big spot for a particular tile, with no backup available if your opponent kills the opening. And frequently you'll have a spot or two, but not have the other necessary tiles to capitalize on it (if you had the tiles already then you'd probably just play it in the first place).

In the previous example, a more plausible scenario would be that you have the **Q** but no **I** or other key letters to go with it. That's where tile tracking comes in. On this occasion there are only two more **I**s to come, so odds are against picking one up. What about if you held **QA** or **QT** and were hoping for **QAT** too? Well there are four **A**s and two **T**s unseen. What about **U**? Only two of those left. Having a number of different tiles to hit and knowing how many of them are left play a massive role in more simple situations like this, where it is much easier to identify which letters you need to draw.

When you're handling **Q** leaves, the situation is likely to be more specific, one where the possible outcomes are much more limited. This is generally also the case when playing off a single tile (*fishing*). A top player could go through the alphabet of unseen letters in a few minutes or less and work out which ones would provide a bonus. Other times it could be that you're hoping to hit a large score, but need a word that includes a particular letter in a certain place, and you can see some words that fit if you draw the right tiles.

Opening Play

Every game of Scrabble has to start somewhere. The first word laid down must go through the centre square. That sounds pretty simple, but there is a lot more to it in practice. I have once actually been in a situation where my opponent managed to place their move a row below the centre square, during a tournament game streamed online in Malta. It wasn't due to ignorance of the rules of course; just a bit of carelessness. I wish I could say I hesitated and felt bad about challenging off their stray word, but I didn't. The first move of the game is unique, as it is almost always negative from a strategic point of view to put the first word on the board. More awkward and defensive options are the least damaging strategically, and in extreme cases have a positive tactical value. Opening plays that give little away typically involve letters that are hard or impossible to parallel, such as **C** and **V**, whilst also not having many, if any, hooks.

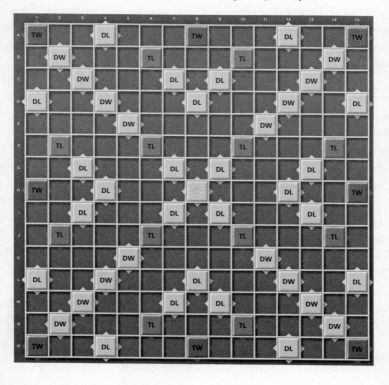

*Some classic blocky opening words would be **VAV**, **VAC**, **GUV**, **VLY**. But be aware of hooks, **VUG** (anagram of **GUV**), for instance, can be extended to **VUG-G** and **VUG-H**, as well as **VUG-S**. Four letters can extend **CAVE** and six letters can hook **COVE**, making them a lot less defensive.*

All of this makes exchanging tiles more viable here than it is in the rest of the game. But it is never worth passing in the hope of getting the letter(s) you need to play an eight-letter word, as a wise or experienced player will simply exchange in response, and will keep doing so until they get a bonus. Be aware, though, that depending on how and where you are playing the game, it may end after six consecutive scores of zero (this can be through changing, passing, or a move challenged off). Games can and have been won minus six to minus eight after the tile values on the racks have been deducted from the scores. In that instance, a cunning player held six one-pointers and a blank, then passed on their third move in the knowledge they would at worst draw the game.

Another slight curiosity about the opening play is you can play horizontally or vertically. It makes no difference either way due to the board symmetry. Most people make the first move going across the board just because it's more natural to do so. A few people have hypothesized that it is fractionally easier to spot eight letter words through the floating tiles provided if the first word is horizontal, so they start vertically. Personally, I don't think it matters, and to simplify things in this section I'm going to ignore starting plays going down the board and stick with horizontal moves.

The usual principles of score and leave still apply to the opening play, but it is often better to exchange one or two tiles if you are close to a bonus but do not have a decent scoring option, such as when you have a set of low value tiles. Playing off a number of bonus-friendly tiles significantly increases the chance of your opponent replying with a bonus, and also makes it easier for them to score with clunky tiles via a parallel play.

E I L N N R T

Promising set of tiles but no bonus. It only actually goes with one tile to make an eight-letter word (I'll let you try to find it). As explained earlier, passing in the hope of getting it is never the right option. Many players would simply throw down a five- or six-letter word with this rack, but this is a classic example where the nuances of an opening play make it better to change. With such friendly-looking tiles you would want to minimize the volatility by keeping as many of them as you can. Keeping **EINRT** (changing **LN**) is the best option here. The **L** doesn't combine well with these tiles, and the other **N** is a duplicate and similarly hinders the rack. The remaining five letters all provide a nicely balanced rack, no duplicates and good synergy. A good chance of having a bonus next turn.

A E E I N R S

An infamous "nearly rack", it goes with most floating tiles to create an eight, but there are no sevens here. The best move is to change an **E** because you will be so likely to have a bonus next turn. Exchanging or playing **AE/EA** isn't too bad either. Volatility is something to avoid when you have such bonus friendly letters, so playing or exchanging three or more tiles here is horrible, because what you pick up is so likely to ruin your rack and prevent you from getting a bonus.

E G L O O S V

This one emphasizes the unique impact of the opening move. **GLOVE** at H4a for twenty-two is, in terms of raw score and leave, superior to **GOV** at H7a for fourteen. However, in actuality **GOV** is the better play by a distance, because it gives so little away. It also provides an **S** hook which is certain to be unspoilt by any parallel play.

A I P R T T W

This is a fairly typical opening rack. There are some duplicates and clunky letters to sort out, so the priority is to play off one of the **T**s and the **W**. There are a variety of options that do this, a few of which use the **P** as well, which will bag some more points.

The best of the bunch include the Scrabble classic **TWP** (sixteen points), a Welsh word for dim-witted. Along a similar theme is **TWIRP** (twenty-six with the **P** on the DL), and thirdly the somewhat more poetic **WRAPT** (twenty-eight with the W on the DL). Because **TWP** is so awkward to reply to and the rack leave of **AIRT** is reasonably nice, it is as good an option as the words scoring ten and twelve points more. Some other options that you may have considered are **PAW**, **WIT**, **TWIT**. The problem with **PAW** is it leaves you with the duplicate **T**s. **WIT** and **TWIT** are quite nice, but don't score enough to compete with the alternatives.

This brings us to some other little factors to think about. When you've found a word you want to play, where do you position it? In the previous example, **WRAPT** or **TWIRP** are simple because one position scores six or four points more respectively than the others. But if there's less of a score differential, then there are a number of other small factors that can dictate the best position. These aren't worth spending much time worrying about, but are worth a moment for consideration during a game.

The first thing most people will consider on their opening move is how their word lines up with the double letter scores (DLs) below and above the middle row. A vowel or **Y** between a pair of DLs typically makes it a lot easier for an opponent to get a pointy letter where it hurts. A lot of the time this will also leave the remainder of the pair of DLs open to a similarly reasonable score. So while it generally goes against you it's not completely one-sided.

ZOO underneath **HIT** would score 48 points, also making (**BI**)**Z** and (**T**)**O**.

The next concerns are which hooks the word takes and what lane they will play in. The columns either side of the centre square, 7 and 9, are not going to give away a great deal of points with a pair of DLs, particularly to longer plays. Next out are 6 and 10 with the triple letter scores, a bit more dangerous generally. 5 and 11 are the innermost double word score lanes, where a bonus in the perfect spot will do a lot of damage, taking in two double word scores. While you'd be unlucky to be hit by a double-double, it's still a good lane to score from if you dangle a word that's easy to hook, and in this case you'd ideally want to funnel plays into the 7 and 9 lanes. Columns further out don't generally impact the choice very often. Avoid creating a big scoring hook for the DLs at H4 and H12. Columns 3 and 13 are generally less damaging than 2 and 14.

If your opponent has a **Z**, your chances are on the fritz.

Once in a blue moon there's an interesting dilemma over whether to play a seven letter word to the extreme left or right of the board, one away from the triple word score. It's a nice dilemma to have. This cropped up in my first ever tournament win in Newcastle-upon-Tyne. My opening rack was **DEIIORZ**, which makes the word **IODIZER** (noun, one who treats with iodine or iodide), a word which coincidentally had been played in the previous game. So I could play it at H8a for a cool 104 points but risk giving a huge score straight back to an **S** (**IODIZERS** alone would score fifty-four points), or choose the safe option at H2a for a mere eighty-eight points. I took the eighty-eight points and was immediately hit back by a bonus ending in a blank **S**.

Of course the fact that I would have been 30–40 points worse off had I played the more aggressive position does not make it the wrong move.

It is important not to judge plays purely on what happened immediately after them, unless of course you're a psychic, in which case I congratulate you on winning the next World Scrabble Championship. The eighty-eight point positioning is better because the odds of getting that huge score are in your opponent's favour, because they get first crack at it and you already have a big lead. With a nice lead, risk and volatility are not your friend. Only in specific circumstances would I advise playing the more aggressive placement. If, for whatever reason, you needed to win the game by a big margin, then gambling works in your favour. Another situation would be that you think your play sets up a hook your opponent will not know or spot.

> *For instance, starting* **ETHANOL** *at H2a on the extreme left. The* **M** *hook making* **METHANOL** *is quite subtle and easy to miss. Similarly, you might get away with* **PRINCES** *to* **PRINCESS** *at H8a. I've managed to sneak through with* **MIKRONS** *(mikron, noun, unit of length) at B8a and later extend it to* **OMIKRONS** *(omikron, noun, Greek letter). For something more exotic there's* **UAKARIS** *at H2a, which can be lengthened to* **OUAKARIS***, both of which are short tailed monkeys, plural form.*

The third and final reason is if your opponent is a far stronger player and you believe rolling the dice and leaving it to chance provides a better chance of victory than the alternative. But of course after reading through all of this you'll be thrashing Scrabble Champions and mere mortals alike, so you won't need any luck.

The last factor to consider when placing your opening move is bonuses or similarly long words going through the floating tiles you have provided, or seven-letter bonuses playing parallel to part of your play. For instance, an **S** on the centre square is going to make it a lot easier for a bonus word to hit the triple word score, most likely a word ending in the **S** but also starting with the **S** too. **E** is a fairly dangerous tile there too, as are **D**, **G**, **R**, and **T**. The other major bonus lane to think about is through columns 5 and 11, the double-double lanes. Vowels here are the most likely to allow a double-double play, but one-point consonants aren't too far behind. In practice, there's often very little one can do to minimize these particular bonus lane dangers.

Opening or obscuring lanes for seven-letter bonuses is the easier thing to do something about. In a lot of cases, the first play will typically just take an **S** hook, occasionally not. So if a seven-letter bonus doesn't hook the first word, then it needs to go parallel to it or it will be homeless. That's a lot of points that may or may not go down. This is again where blocky letters come into play, and these have good utility on the opening move. Have a quick thought about common endings for sevens, such as -**S**, -**ING**, -**ED**, -**ER**, and whether your opening move would stop those going down. The starts of sevens are harder to imagine, but think about words starting with a consonant-vowel or consonant-vowel-vowel pattern. Placing your opening move to the left of the board will typically force any potential bonus word to the right side, and vice versa.

| A | A | L | S | U | W | |

This is actually an opening rack from a game in a 24 Hour Challenge. I had the pleasure of facing off against thirty different opponents across twenty-four hours, with a mere ten minutes to play my whole game. After having a somewhat hasty look for bonuses (there aren't any), there is one root word that stood out, which is **WAUL** (verb, to cry like a cat, as in caterwaul). In actuality I played **WAULS** at H4a for twenty-four keeping **A?**. I wasn't too bothered about the **S** on the centre square because I had the blank, so had a good shot at using it. **WAUL** or **WAULS** are roughly the same on further evaluation, because the **S** is so strong and evens out the vowel.

So, if you decide on **WAUL**, where do you put it? Well, you can't avoid putting a vowel between a pair of DLs. The **A** is a bigger danger than the **U** because there are many more two-letter words with an **A**. But on the plus side, we have the **S**, so leaving the **S** hook for **WAUL** in a useful position is to our advantage, because that's probably where we'll lay our bonus next move, unless we're unlucky. H5a is pretty good defensively, but leaves our -**S** hook in the least favourable position. H6a and H8a are a bit more open to pointy parallel plays, with the **A** in the juicy spots, but puts our -**S** hook lane in a better column. The best option is H7a, which combines good defence with a nice lane for our **S** next move.

Moving On

After the first word goes down, there aren't really any more intricacies to worry about in the early stages of a game. Whether it is the second or the eighth move of the game, they will all follow the same reasoning. The board is nearly always open to bonus plays and it is almost impossible to shut the game down completely. Having more awkward letters on the leftmost side of the board may make it difficult to use the top left corner, but there will still generally be accessible areas of the board elsewhere.

Scoreboard strategy is generally not a factor, and because of the open nature of the early stages, difficult to implement anyway. Not enough tiles have been played to skew the letter bag one way or another, so tile tracking is not a significant consideration. From my perspective, the first half a dozen moves for each player (the opening play excepted) are the most robotic. It's almost purely score and leave, with little thought to anything else, because the game hasn't really taken shape yet. It can also be a frustrating part of the contest, because you can be rendered powerless with terrible racks whilst your opponent hits you with two or three bonuses and rides off into the sunset. Everyone gets blitzed like this occasionally.

Inference

I remember the days when poker was a game more associated with the Wild West, a somewhat private pursuit mainly enjoyed by gents characterized by their levels of inebriety and infamy. It isn't really my sort of scene, though I nevertheless enjoyed watching the drama unfold in films and television before it really took off as the multi-billion pound industry it is now. One of my earliest memories is of an episode of the BBC television classic *Only Fools and Horses* where Del Boy outcheats Boycie with his 'two pair' – a pair of aces and another pair of aces.

Watching TV programs such as Late Night Poker, seeing poker players in the days before they became big brands and celebrities in front of my eyes, I was always intrigued by a number of things about the game. I have always loved to be part of a big event. Poker has these in almost unlimited supply, and I looked on with envy, wishing they existed on the same scale in Scrabble. I'm always available if a company wants me to endorse them for a few million. I have a lot of appreciation for the skills involved in poker, keeping emotions in check, and the maths side of things, being the numbers guy I am. These are valuable in Scrabble too, but another important skill in poker I want to discuss is inference

Inference is defined as the act or process of deriving conclusions from information you believe to be true. Almost every player at some point uses inference, perhaps without even really being aware of what they're doing. For instance, when an opponent creates a huge spot for an **S**, scoring next to nothing in the process, most players would automatically assume they have an **S** to use it next turn. It introduces a little bit of detective work and bluff into the game – maybe they don't have the **S** and want us to block it?

The higher the standard of opponent, the more reliable inference generally is. Each move from your opponent gives you some clues, even if it's only a mere hint about the strength of their rack leave. But it's also important to state that it is not an exact science. It is easy to whip yourself into a frenzy worrying that everything your opponent does is some devilish setup which they will soon hit you with next turn. Perspective is key.

You are perhaps wondering why the opponent's skill makes the inference more reliable? Well, you will often get false tells if you look purely at what has just been played. Using inference in this way means you are heavily reliant on your opponent making the best play. A mistake can provide misinformation. However, you may find other clues are more forthcoming. A blank or two tends to slow a lot of players down, likewise a rack that looks particularly likely to yield a bonus, but one can't be found. There are also the more poker-esque inference skills of course, such as body language, facial expression whilst revealing tiles, the odd grumble, staring at a particular area of the board, and a vacant, disinterested look (often associated with an all consonant/vowel rack, or when my partner takes me shoe shopping). Another important thing to mention is that sometimes telegraphing you have a particular tile (generally an **S**) can throw your opponent's game out, because they worry about it too much. Top Scrabblers know that keeping a second **S** doesn't generally improve the rack much, so they play it off when it only nets the odd extra point. A lot of players pick up on it and then play too defensively.

Inference is undoubtedly a good skill to have though, despite the pitfalls. It is generally peripheral to the game and a distant second to factors like scoring, leave, and general strategy. Most of the time, you're getting little snippets of information which don't really alter your choice. But once in a while, particularly at the highest level, it can make the difference between winning and losing.

Here are a couple of high-level sequences which are particularly intriguing, both from the 2013 World Scrabble Championship final between Nigel Richards and Komol Panyasoponlert.

DUH has just been played at J4a and you're sitting with an indifferent rack, a good few points behind. What can you read into the previous play, and how can you use it to your advantage?

Well, **DUH** scored pretty well, thirty-eight points to be exact. So that doesn't tell us a great deal. There aren't any other obvious spots for the **H**, and there's not much flexibility to substitute other letters into that play. There are no **H**s or **P**s left to play **HUH** or **PUH** for slightly more points. There is one key piece of information though: they could have swapped the **H** out for an **X**. If they had an **X**, they would surely have played **DUX** for another twenty-four points, so they presumably don't have it. What now? There's no great move to play on the board. But we know that, unless our opponent drew the **X** after playing **DUH**, we can create an opening for it. **EL** can be hooked with

B, **P**, or **T** to make **BEL**, **PEL**, or **TEL** respectively. Nigel made a great inference play here of **TIP** at G5a for sixteen. It threatens a big **X** play which can turn the game, so the opponent has to do something about it.

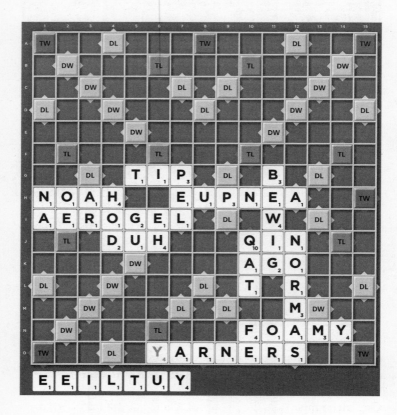

Following on, our opponent, in this case Nigel (a player known for creating ingenious setups) has just put **TIP** down. With no tiles to really score with on the triple letter score, what do you play?

The opening can't be left unobscured because an **X** will score fifty points or more, so it leaves a dilemma. It is easy to block but how much score and leave is sacrificed in the process? It is hard to say what is the right option. Ultimately Komol played **YULE** at F2a for seventeen, killing the **X** spot. It was the best score-and-leave play, but it created a big double-double bonus lane at E5a which could be far more devastating.

Funnily enough, in the game Nigel actually picked the **X** after creating the setup and scored thirty-eight for VOX at E5a, whilst Komol drew a bonus.

One last example from the 2013 final. Our opponent has played the highly suspicious (**J**)**EU** at K6d for ten. The word takes an **X**. A word stretching from the double word score using the **X** would score nearly 100 points. An obvious setup? Perhaps too obvious. Maybe they're just dumping a couple of vowels.

It is elementary to take out the **X** spot completely, but then it sacrifices score. Not to mention there's a triple word score open at H1a as well. What if you can score *and* obscure the **X** spot? There are basically two options here: playing **CAM** at N7a for sixteen or **MAC** at M7d for thirty-five.

Is completely defeating the **X** spot worth nineteen points? This one is more clear-cut. **MAC** for thirty-five blocks the spot in a way that the vast majority of the time it is unusable. An opponent scoring an extra thirty points or so on the odd occasion averages out to far less than nineteen.

In the game itself Komol responded to Nigel's setup by playing **MAC** at M7d for thirty-five. Nigel just happened to have the perfect letters to slot in **EX(A)CT** at N5a for seventy-three. Sometimes the right play has the wrong result. Without the **A** making things awkward, Nigel could have played **CORTEX** for ninety-six, so in this instance it at least mitigated some of the damage.

The thing to remember, though, is that this is extremely high-level play, the sort that rarely crops up even in World Championship games, let alone anywhere else. The vast majority of the time, just playing normally is best and the odd bit of information gleaned from inference won't influence what the best play is, unless the choice is a marginal one. When it does matter, though, it's pretty amazing to watch, and it brings a different dimension to the game.

General Play

This section covers the bulk of the game, basically from the second move onwards: the bread-and-butter situations of every match. They set the scene for later stages. As a match progresses, the board generally becomes tighter, and things like score and unseen tiles have a much greater role in proceedings.

The positions that follow will be mostly about score and leave, but other minor factors will influence things a little here and there. See if you can put into practice what you've learnt so far.

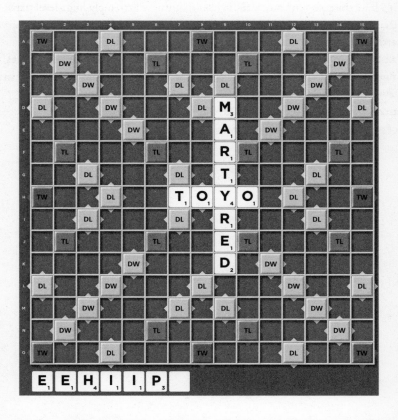

Only a couple of moves have been played. Things are looking up with the blank on the rack, but two pairs of vowels are hampering things somewhat.

After a good look, there are no bonuses available here, so now we're looking for other plays. The spot at D8 looks inviting for the **H**. Unfortunately we can't reach the triple word score without burning a blank. Something like **PITH** A8d for forty-seven would be a horrible move, because it leaves you with **EEI**, which means the move overall is only worth in the region of thirty-five points. The blank and a couple of reasonable tiles are virtually worth that sitting on the rack before you even score anything. There is actually quite a cool play of **IMPHEE** (an African sorghum plant) at A8d for fifty-seven, but it's still not the best play here.

Because we're at such an early stage on a wide open board, the blank is a bit better on your rack than it would typically be. So playing **I(M)PHEE** for twenty-eight through the **M** in **MARTYRED** and keeping **I?** does comfortably better than burning the blank for the extra twenty-nine points. There is one final spot that looks quite inviting: the triple letter score at J10. The **H** can play down from there and score well. Playing **HIE** there is the best play. It scores thirty and keeps **EIP?**. **HI** in the same spot is arguably the second-best move in this situation, but indisputably worse than **HIE** because of the vowel balance and duplication.

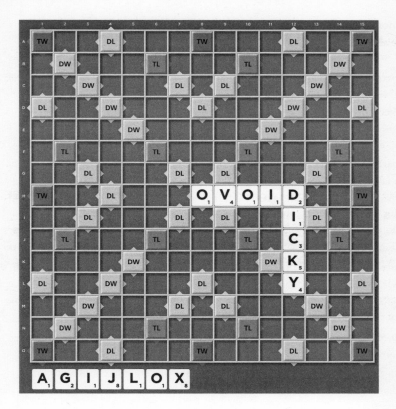

A clunky rack, but it should be reasonable for scoring. The board, however, isn't great for power tiles with no nooks to get juicy parallel plays going. Lets have a look at a few options.

I think we can safely say there's no bonus available. Next up, lets break the rack down. Ideally we'd like to play off the **J** as the weaker of the two biggies. The **G** is a bit awkward, particularly with the **X**. There are a few dumps like **AJI** at L13d for twenty-five, but that's pretty inviting for a big counterplay, and leaves quite an awkward **GLOX**. **AX** or **AXIL** in the same spot has similar issues. It sets up a **J** dump in column 14 using **YA-G**, but that's relatively slim pickings compared to the likely damage sustained. There's the simple (**C**)**OX** at J12a for twenty-eight. It leaves **AGIJL**, which is moderate, and sets up (**COX**)**A** for next turn, but with eight As unseen from eighty-four tiles, more often than not our opponent will use it. (**COX**)**Y**, meaning 'cocky', is also a possibility, so that furthers the risk.

Another option would be the fairly simply **JA**(**K**) at K10a for twenty-eight. It's a good score, but a somewhat awkward leave of **GILOX**. Overall a strong choice though. It's a shame **JAX**(**Y**) at L9a only scores a face value twenty-one, one of those moves where the points don't match the aesthetics.

At E11 we can fit in **GOJ**(**I**) (another name for wolfberry, the berry of particular plants) for twenty-four, which looks quite promising. It opens up a lane for an **X** play in column 12, which is pretty handy, but nothing spectacular. **GAJO** and **GOJI** can play at G7a and I7a. Keeping the **A** back is a little better. Normally the higher placement would be better defensively, despite it being marginally easier to bonus off; however, we're holding the **X**, and opening up a potential fifty or more point play is certainly to our advantage. So of all the options I prefer **GOJI** at I7a for twenty-two. It also has defensive merit, in that it would prevent a lot of seven-letter bonuses going down above or below the **O** in **OVOID**.

This position doesn't really have a clear-cut best play, and probably comes down to your own personal style, as well as your opponent. A weaker opponent is more likely to play through a triple letter score, and **JA**(**K**) could end up being better in that scenario. If you had any inference information, that could also sway what is a marginal choice.

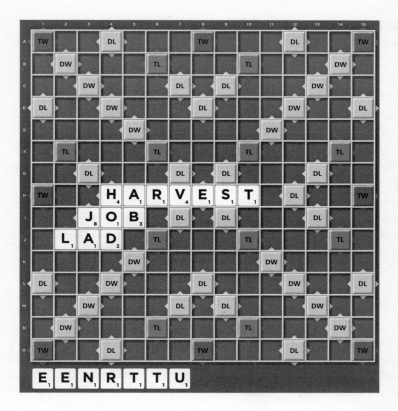

So, a rack with potential. I'll save you the trouble of looking too hard and tell you that there isn't a bonus here. The rack would, however, have combined with a floating **B**, **F**, or **H** (all common words). There aren't many ways to score with this rack. Extending **JOB** to **JOBE** (verb, to extensively rebuke) is the most flexible. Next is extending **LAD** to **LADE**, and in the process forming a word around **AB**. Then finally there's extending **JA** to the double word score.

There are a lot of nice leaves possible with this rack, but nothing too amazing because of the **U** and duplicate tiles. So a few good options would be **(R)ET** H6d for eighteen leaving **ENRTU**, or the more obscure **U(R)ENT** at G6d for twenty, keeping **ERT**. Similarly there's **(AB)ET** at H5d for seventeen – this one has the disadvantage of creating an extra hook in the first column.

LAD takes **B**, **C**, and **G**. **LADE** curiously takes the same hooks, plus **S**. Turning over two tiles makes it unlikely we'll catch one of them.

The final place to look for leaves is the **JA**. That can be extended to (**JA**)**NTEE** and (**JA**)**UNTEE**, which are both variations of 'jaunty'. Lastly, there's (**JA**)**UNT**, which can be a noun or a verb (to go on a jaunt; a pleasurable trip). (**JA**)**UNTEE**, scoring twenty-eight, actually does quite well in analysis. Getting rid of the **U** is important so (**JA**)**NTEE** does badly. The star of the show, though, is (**JA**)**UNT** at I3d for twenty-four and a strong keep of **EERT**, which at worst is only a little behind any other rack leave here.

Okay, so lets summarize. This rack has great potential: no duplicates, but vowel heavy. The **Y** is a hindrance, and after confirming there is no bonus play available, you'd be looking to play the **Y** off with a vowel or two and score. With regards to the board, it's in the early stages. There's a flexible scoring spot at F9/10, dangerous if your opponent has a **Z**, but then there are eighty other tiles unseen, so the chances of them having it are less than 1 in 10. The scoreline doesn't really matter at this stage.

DAPPER does actually take an **S**, because it has another meaning as a fish bait. There's also **S(JOE)** available. So the board has bonus lanes for an **S**. Now where can we use the **Y** and score? Well, **OX(Y)** is possible, but **AEIOST** is still way too vowel-heavy to be a strong leave. We'll discount that. We're aiming to dump a vowel or two with the **Y**. The **O** is the next weakest link. **YO** and **OY** play in a number of places. The standout play is **YO** at I8a for thirty. A very powerful leave with the added bonus of another -**S** bonus lane. To put it into context the next best plays are also **YO** or **OY**.

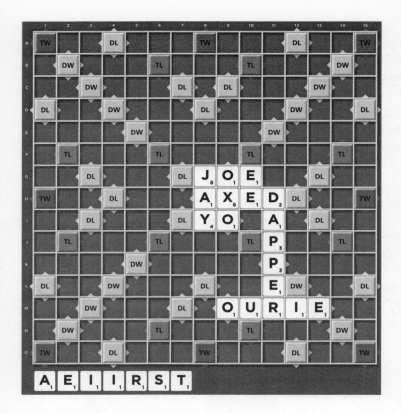

Our opponent has played **OU(R)IE**, a Scottish adjective meaning 'gloomy' It can be compared, so **OURIER** and **OURIEST** are also valid. For us an annoying duplicate, but it looks promising for a bonus.

Without too much shuffling **AIRIEST** is available. This also has the more obscure anagram **IRISATE**, a verb meaning to make iridescent. So where is the best place to play a bonus?

IRISATE only actually plays at N3a for a pitiful sixty-one points. **AIRIEST** will slot in to the right at N4a for sixty-seven, as well as above **OURIE** at L3a for sixty-eight. Close call right? Well, not if you keep looking. Hopefully you've found the eighty-four point placement, at B7d. If you were all set to weigh up the lesser options, then you need to always be aware of slotting words in like this. Be thorough and look everywhere.

Rack: A₁ B₃ D₂ M₃ N₁ O₁ T₁

A bit further on in the same game. Loads of decent options here scoring in the 20s or early 30s and leaving something reasonable. Now lets show the unseen tiles:

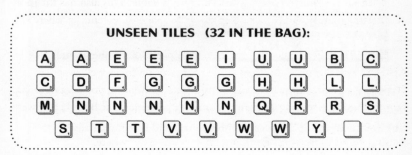

UNSEEN TILES (32 IN THE BAG):

A₁ A₁ E₁ E₁ E₁ I₁ U₁ U₁ B₃ C₃

C₃ D₂ F₄ G₂ G₂ G₂ H₄ H₄ L₁ L₁

M₃ N₁ N₁ N₁ N₁ Q₁₀ R₁ R₁ S₁

S₁ T₁ T₁ V₄ V₄ W₄ W₄ Y₄ ☐

So what's the best play? Before you factor in the unseen tiles, the best two moves would have comfortably ranked outside the top 20. With so few vowels, the spot at L12 becomes important, not only to dump consonants and score, but also to prevent your opponent from doing likewise. Also note the high number of **N**s left. So the best options are now **N(I)MB** and **M(I)ND**, both at L12d, both scoring twenty-six. They preserve vowels and play off the **N** which could be problematic in future turns.

Here we have a pretty ropey rack. Our opponent has just played **OO** at D12d for sixteen. There's a nice open triple letter score at J6; however, we can't do much with it. Next turn, though, it could become an ally.

What does the play of **OO** tell us? Clearly, they have a pretty good rack leave – certainly one that's better than ours. It is likely to be bonus-friendly, and probably includes all single-pointers. Why? Because they had that juicy triple letter score open and left it. Given they've only played off two tiles, they could be keeping something particularly strong and may be odds-on to bonus next go. Ordinarily the triple letter score at J6 would be a little bit of a worry, but not too big a concern. It's an easily accessible spot to dump pointy tiles, particularly the **X**, obviously. It is the flexibility and the relatively dead board elsewhere (other than for bonuses) that make it more of a factor now. There's also **OATY**, of course, which takes the **G**. With two left in a moderate position, that's nothing to be concerned about.

Getting back to our opponent's rack leave: given the inference, it is to our advantage to leave ways to score with short plays. With only two tiles drawn, they're unlikely to draw pointy stuff and hit us with it. We can be aggressive in that respect, but try and be defensive when it comes to bonus lanes, or at least not open anything up. For instance, at C13d we would want to avoid playing **KINO**, because the **O** makes it a lot easier for bonuses to play in column 14 by hooking the **O**. So if we swap the **K** and **O** round, then we have **OINK** in the same spot, which is stronger. There's a nice play from C11a, the onomatopoeic (**C**)**LUNK** for twenty-five. It leaves a fairly weak **INO**. Placing the **K** in the triple lane is fine because it's not a bonus-friendly tile, but it would allow our opponent to balance their rack if they're vowel-heavy (which is more likely) or have other one pointers, and score twenty-one or more in the process. Providing a floating **N** in an early position shouldn't be overly useful for bonuses. **CLUNK** does make accessing column 13 a lot harder, so that's a plus.

There's one last choice I want to talk about, which is playing **UNLINK** at A13d for twenty-nine. A lot of players would shy away from playing this. They'd be worried about the nine-timer or the potential of a cheap **Q** play. If we assume our opponent doesn't have a **Q**, and I think that's almost certainly the case here, then they have about a 3 per cent chance of drawing it. The odds of a triple-triple are significantly less still, because the **U** is a bad tile in an awkward place. The implied odds of a bonus are more like 50 per cent, maybe higher.

Ultimately, Scrabble is a risk and reward game. Turning over six tiles gives us a better chance than our opponent of getting power tiles to do damage with, or a clunky rack to score with and hopefully balance for later. If we're lucky, we might draw a bonus ourselves. This is the sort of aggressive play that I see regularly at the top level, particularly in the early stages of a game. Playing passively and conservatively doesn't really work, because an opponent will still get big moves down, and it only ends up stunting your own scoring chances.

This is a position from an online consensus game, where a group on Facebook played against top Australian Scrabbler David Eldar. David has just played **ODEA** (plural of 'odeum', a concert hall) in the top-right hand corner, but he still trails by thirty-three points. First off, what can we read from the play? Well David clearly didn't have an **N**, otherwise a player of his caliber would have played **ANODE/ION/OXO/BED/GONE** in the same area. This isn't particularly useful information though.

A more general inference is David is vowel-heavy, or has just balanced his rack. He is highly unlikely to have kept three consonants because he could simply have played **ODE**, kept the **A** back and retained a much better, more balanced rack. We have a significant enough lead that the main way back for David is to get a bonus play and the main way for us to win is to restrict his options, but also ideally to try and increase the lead such that even a bonus play is not enough for David to win.

Looking at the board, there are three main areas to bonus. **HOTEN** is a past participle of 'hete', to command. This word cannot be extended. **DUI**, the plural of 'duo', can only be extended with a **T** to form **DUIT**, an old Dutch coin. Two **T**s have been played and we have two more on our rack. This means there are two unseen. Playing across and hooking **DUI** with one/both of the remaining **T**s is one place where David can bonus (he could also play down the right of **GASSIER** but it's very awkward). The two remaining places are more obvious spots: an eight-letter word through the **B**, **R**, and **A** in **BRAVA** in the top left, and along the rightmost lane. The last is the most dangerous, because most seven-letter words will play there and will generally be high scoring.

Purely in terms of score and leave, the best option is **PA(R)TAKE** in the top left corner for thirty-two points, leaving a solitary **T**. With a different scoreline, such as us being significantly behind, this would be a great move because it is open and volatile. It leaves us with a **T** for the **DUI** hook, the **P** to play through in the top left corner, and finally sevens down the rightmost lane. Draw that unseen blank, which is more likely when turning over six tiles, and it will be very difficult to stop us getting a bonus. Drawing six random tiles also means we could pick something absolutely horrible whilst our opponent hits us with big scores. This volatility and openness works against us when we're ahead.

We also need to consider some some plays down that right lane onto the triple word score. A few of the better options are **TAK** (a Scottish word meaning "take", twenty-three points), **TAKE** and **TEAK** (both for twenty-six), and finally **APEAK** (meaning in a vertical position, thirty-five). The first three words help balance our rack by removing the duplicate **T**, but **APEAK** scores a lot more. A word ending in **K** prevents any sort of bonus playing down the right hand side, whereas **TAKE** allows most bonuses to play alongside the **E**. So we can rule out **TAKE** in favour of **TEAK**, because it's essentially the same, but the latter blocks up that lane.

If there were a dearth of **E**s and other vowels, then we would perhaps favour **TAK** over **TEAK**, sacrificing three points to keep the **E**. That isn't the case here. So we're left with **TEAK** versus **APEAK**. **TEAK** scores twenty-six, leaving **APT**. **APEAK** scores thirty-five, leaving **TT**. **APT** is a better rack leave than **TT**, but is it nine points better?

Turning over another tile helps the game end a little quicker, so that is in our favour, given we're leading. A nice, balanced leave of **APT** gives us some insurance against drawing all consonants or all vowels. But we'd be very unlucky to pick five consonants when leaving **TT**, and indeed for each time that happened there would be as many times where we pick the blank with our extra turnover – which would make us a massive favourite. **A**, **P**, and **T** aren't particularly useful tiles individually, and they don't combine well, as there are two hard consonants. Ultimately, there's a lot of volatility whether we're picking four or five tiles, so that restricts how good or bad a leave will be. So keeping **APT** or **TT** doesn't make a difference of nine points. Other factors making the leave less significant are that we're on a tightish board and we're trying to block it up further, so there's less opportunity to cash in good tiles for big points and more emphasis placed on scoring immediately. Pushing our lead up to sixty-eight with **APEAK** edges us up to a point where a bonus from David is frequently not enough. He may also have to sacrifice points to open the board up.

Other Strategies

So far we've seen a lot of situations. Score and leave have dominated the discussion, but other considerations have come into play. I wanted to discuss further tactics that come up now and again. As you'll have seen now and again, setups do occasionally come into the equation. These can be deliberate, blatant attempts to open something up. They can also be bluffs, of course, with the aim of thwarting our opponent by getting them to sacrifice equity. A lot of setups are accidental or incidental to the play, however: a case of making a move and then realizing that it happens to tick a few other boxes as well. It isn't important how a player arrives at the fact that a particular move has extra strategical value, so long as it is considered. As well as setups, there are related situations where you can plan ahead. Lets for example imagine you have **ADEFGMO** on your rack. You might look at the board and decide you'd like to play **FOG** somewhere. Elsewhere there might be a decent spot for **MEAD**, which are the tiles you're keeping. so you have that as a backup, whatever tiles you draw. It always helps to have a score guaranteed before you even dip your hand in the bag, or even if it hinges on picking a range of bountiful letters or your opponent not blocking the spot. Something like this helps to overwrite general rack leave evaluations with something that's based on what you know you may actually score – which is much more relevant. Ultimately, leave values are just a guess of how a particular set of tiles is going to affect your average score for the next turn. If you know you're going to get a high score next turn, or at worst a middling one, then that's effectively a good leave.

Another strategy that comes up occasionally is known as a *fork*. This is when one word opens the board up in two places or lanes. A player may specifically look for this sort of play when trailing by a bonus and needing to create two openings at once, so the opposing player can't easily block both. But it happens more often when a player has some scoring power and can't cash in well enough on the current move, so they open up two high scoring spots, knowing they've got the tiles to likely score heavily next turn on whichever one is still open.

Here's a real life example of a fork, played in the second game of the 2014 World Scrabble Championship final between myself and Chris Lipe.

Forks are typically speculative, because you're usually playing off a few tiles and have no idea what you're going to pick up. On this occasion, Chris had just played **HEN**, blocking a juicy **X** spot, and I figured he had quite a good balanced rack, but obviously hadn't kept an **X**. I was leading by fifty-four points and didn't really want to be volatile. However, my best play was undoubtedly **PA(Y)OUT** at N10a for thirty-four. It forked the board and I would get a triple word score whatever happened.

This sort of opening is going to result in plenty of points each way. It's important to remember that you will typically lose out on average if you create two spots that are both accessible. Even more so if one spot is a lot more useful than the other. This is because the opponent gets first choice. This can change, however, if you have relevant inference information, a very strong rack leave, or key tiles that give you effective access to both openings whilst the other player does not.

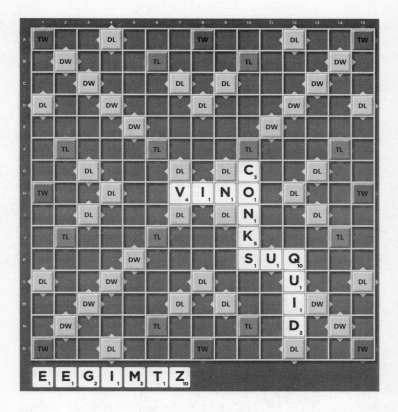

So an opponent has just played **(Q)UID**; you've got no **S**, and there's no fantastic **Z** play. How can you fork the board to your advantage?

Have you spotted it? We can play **MI(D)GE** or **MI(D)GET** at N10a for thirty or thirty-two points respectively. This creates two great triple word score lanes for the **Z**. Personally, I would leave the **T** off. There's still a decent chance your opponent will have a hook for **MIDGE**, but it may force them to burn an **S**, and they may have a better option with the other spot anyway. They may also think you don't have the hook and choose to leave what appears to be the less accessible spot open.

Finally, a quick word about extensions. These can be very difficult to spot, partially because it's so easy to overlook them. I'm basically talking about longer words that are placed on the board that can then be lengthed by two or more letters. So for instance if a player opened with **SHOCK**, with the **S** on the centre square, then it could be extended to (**SHOCK**)**ERS** or (**SHOCK**)**ING**. Lets see if you can find the three extensions on the next board.

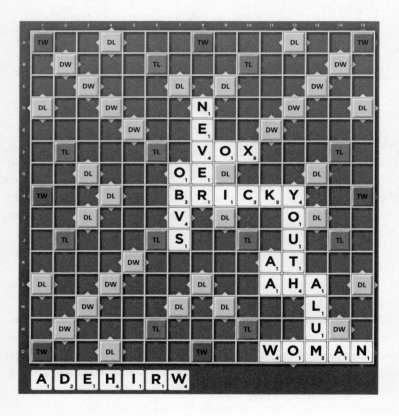

Have you found them yet?

The words are **WHE(NEVER)**, **(BRICKY)ARD** and **AIR(WOMAN)**. Always try and be aware of the possibilities as soon as you see them, even if you don't have the letters.

Late-Game

This chapter generally relates to the phase where there are twenty tiles or less in the bag. Typically, one player is significantly ahead and trying to keep things tight whilst their opponent attempts to do the opposite. Close games obviously don't lend themselves to quite as much out-and-out blocking or opening up. Remaining tiles are generally skewed one way or another. Choosing the best move veers a little bit away from score and leave, as other factors become increasingly significant. The late-game period is much more nuanced and strategic, thinking on your feet is very necessary to properly evaluate the situation.

Each game is a little different but, generally speaking, if you're ahead then high turnover will get the game to a finish more quickly and be in your favour. Turnover can also be crucial if a player is effectively two bonuses ahead. At that stage, if seven tiles or fewer remain in the bag (*pre-endgame*), then if a bonus does happen there either aren't enough letters to draw to get the second bonus or the player bonusing will get the last seven tiles. Those should be known through tile tracking, and a potential second bonus can be blocked unless the rack is flexible enough to allow bonuses in two separate places.

There's another quirk when a game gets to exactly seven tiles in the bag. This is the last time a player can exchange, but also it's often the best time to do so. At this stage there is a tactical bonus to exchanging all seven letters, because whatever tiles were on your rack are about to do a swap with whatever you're taking from the bag. So make sure you actually write down what you're exchanging before you do it. By process of elimination, you also then know what's on your opponent's rack. So when their turn is played you can factor in what tiles they've kept and what pool of letters they're drawing from. This can be very useful information. So if you have to have an atrocious rack, have it when there are seven tiles in the bag.

Turnover is a mixed blessing, however. It means volatility, and this can be good or bad. One of the main ways of overturning a significant deficit at the end is through sticking an opponent with the **Q**. Having unplayable tiles can happen with other tiles too, of course, particularly if the board has become a bit awkward (such as the top left corner being inaccessible).

So drawing more tiles increases the likelihood of getting undesirable letters as well as the good ones, which can kill the game. An overview of what's to come can determine the value of turnover. Remember that, generally speaking, the bag is neutral. That changes during the course of a game. A match can often hinge on who draws a particular tile. If there are two blanks and three **S**s to come with twenty tiles unseen, then the bag becomes pretty positive, as does turnover. Just hope your opponent doesn't have those goodies already.

As mentioned above, the late-game phase when there are seven tiles or less in the bag is known as the pre-endgame. When the bag is empty, the game then moves into the endgame. These are both notoriously difficult to play well in.

The pre-endgame can often involve going through the unseen tiles and looking for potential bonus plays, either for you or your opponent, depending on the scoreline, or perhaps examining other threats such as a big power tile play. Then there's also the old favourite of the **Q** and perhaps hanging onto the appropriate letters for it in case it lands on your rack, or trying to block potential **Q** dumps for your opponent. Sometimes it is just about trying to find a very unlikely way to win, or lose, and acting accordingly.

One of the few rules I hear from competitive Scrabblers is not emptying the bag. And this is quite a good one, but like most things, not always 100 per cent correct. It is generally bad to empty the tile bag, and by this we mean play off the exact amount of tiles that are left to pick up. So if there are three in the bag, avoid playing off three tiles. The reason behind this is your opponent then has knowledge of your full rack, and this makes it a lot easier to block bonuses, big plays etc. It also means they can plan an out-in-two, whilst you also lose out more on countback. Occasionally there's a good reason to empty the bag, but in general it's quite a bad thing to do. Try and leave one or two in the bag instead if it's not going to sacrifice too much. Leaving one behind is best if your opponent is trying for a bonus. Two is sometimes better, such as if there are more open areas to play longer words, and an opponent's out-in-two would be very likely with one in the bag.

The endgame is the most logical part of Scrabble. With exact knowledge of your opponent's rack (at least in theory), it allows for plotting out sequences of plays, countering the other player, setting up big scores, sticking the opponent with a particular tile or tiles, and trying to avoid the same happening to you. Being stuck with letters happens only very occasionally at the top level when the boards are more open. At lower levels, however, the games tend to be a little more congested.

Generally, you're looking to go out as quickly as possible and stop your opponent from doing likewise. This often makes a big difference to the final score, because you're getting an extra move on your opponent, and then the value of the tiles remaining on their rack. Planning your moves out is crucial. It's no good leaving yourself only one place to go out if your opponent blocks it. So having more options is better.

There is no silver bullet when it comes to late-game Scrabble. It is very difficult, and each game is unique. If you're playing with a clock, ensure you have plenty of time left at the end to go through the different processes, check, and double check. This is one area where playing experience really does help everyone over a sustained period of time.

This game is from the 2013 World Scrabble Championships. Northern Ireland's Paul Gallen, ranked one of the best five players worldwide, played Komol Panyasoponlert from Thailand, who went on to finish second in the tournament.

Komol has just played **YIN** at H10d for twenty-four. Paul trails by twenty-two points and has this rack. It is quite well balanced, no duplicates, some good strong letters, with a couple messing up the bonus synergy a little bit, but offering some scoring potential instead. The board is very top-heavy, potentially wide open at the bottom, but the only realistic bonus lane is in column 2. The unseen tiles are skewed towards vowels and clunky tiles. Twelve vowels unseen compared to ten consonants. No **S**s or blanks to come, but the worst of the power tiles left, **J** and **Q**, along with a few hard consonants. Not the prettiest tile pool.

Lets throw out some options, then. There's **FAY** or **FEY** in a couple of places – I11d and D15d. Quite a few plays from I11d: **FYCE**, **FAERY**, **FANCY**, and **FARCY** for instance. You could just play **FY** and leave the very friendly-looking **ACENR**. You could be a bit more conservative and just play off **EF** in the top right corner at C13a.

The plays in column 11 all score quite well. **FAY** is twenty-five, **FAERY** is twenty-nine, **FANCY** and **FARCY** are thirty-three, and **FYCE** is thirty-four. The bonus-friendly leaves are wasted on this board and the remaining tiles, so we'll discount **FY**, which only scores 17/18 points. With all the vowels to come, it favours keeping something more consonant heavy. If we look at the unseen tiles, there's quite big scoring potential in all of the longer column 11 moves. On a board like this, we have to realize that anything we open up is going to heavily influence the game. Looking closer at those plays in column 11 and the unseen tiles, the plays of **FANCY** and **FARCY** are quite dangerous with one **H** unseen out of twenty-two, as it allows a flexible play that scores. But bigger threats lie with words like **QUI(C)H/QUI(C)HE**. **QUICH** is a verb, 'to stir'. **JUI(C)E** would also play, and given there are many **U**s, **I**s, and **E**s left, it is also more likely. The **C** is also a good floater for bonuses. **FANCY** and **FARCY** also leave us only one consonant with loads of vowels to come, so we'll rule those out.

FAERY at I11d doesn't score quite so much and provides an arguably even more useful **R** floater, allowing big scores like **QUI(R)E** and **JIR(R)E** to play, as well as bonuses. It doesn't give much up to parallel plays, however, and holding the **C** back is quite useful in this scenario, with vowels to come, as well as combining nicely with the **Q**. **FYCE** only sticks out a floating **E**, which, with a vowel heavy bag and our rack leave, isn't a big problem. There are a few **Q/J** threats (**QUI(E)T**, **QUE(E)N**, **QUE(E)R**, **JAG(E)R** etc.), but they all include letters which are scarcer among the unseen. Parallels off the **E** are easier, but don't do much damage. The keep of **ANR** is quite nice, even given the bag. It's just a shame about the four **A**s remaining.

> **QUIRE** *verb, to arrange paper in sets of twenty-four*
> **JIRRE** *an exclamation of surprise or admiration*
> **JAGER** *noun, also jaeger, a German or Austrian marksman*

We'll discount **FEY**, as with four **A**s to come you'd much rather play **FAY**. The position at I11d doesn't really give much away, so considering the extra three points, we'll look at that position rather than D15d. The main virtue of **FAY** is it leaves a strong **CENR**, which combines well with the vowelly bag. A solid option.

Now let's think about what our opponent can do already, and if there's anything worthwhile that reduces the threat. In column 2 there's potential for a bonus, or something like **EQUINE**. There's a cute little play of (**E**)**NE** at H1 for seventeen, which would block those options and leave FARCY on our rack to play at I11d next turn. Of course, if our opponent has **EQUINE** he could also play it at H13 and score broadly as much.

Speaking of H13, there are a few **Q** plays from there that could do substantial damage, such as (**E**)**QUATE**, (**E**)**QUINIA**, (**E**)**QUALI**. There's another dinky play that would disrupt them: **NA**(**E**) at F13d for sixteen. It leaves **CEFRY**.

> **FARCY** *noun, a form of glanders (disease in horses)*
> **EQUINIA** *noun, another name for glanders*
> **EQUALI** *plural noun, pieces for a group of instruments of the same kind*
> **MAHA** *noun, a form of yoga*
> **MIHA** *noun, a young fern frond which has not yet opened*
> **MIHI** *verb, to greet as in the Maori ceremonial greeting*

Those are nice little moves, but don't score enough to be serious considerations.

So that's the main choices done and dusted. After flogging the computer the results are in... analysis favours **FYCE** at I11d. The likes of **FAY** aren't too far behind, though. **FARCY** is a little better than **FANCY** due to not allowing parallel plays with the **M** and **H** (**MAHA**, **MIHA**, **MIHI**). Very difficult one to call even with time and technology on your hands. In the actual game Paul played **FANCY** at I11d for thirty-three.

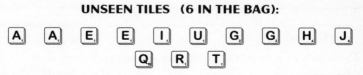

UNSEEN TILES (6 IN THE BAG):

A A E E I U G G H J Q R T

A continuation of the Paul v Komol game. After Paul's **FANCY**, Komol dumped **EUOI** at C15 for eleven, and we've got **AAELMNR** to ponder over. It's safe to say **EUOI** implies vowel heaviness, and almost certainly no big tile to go with it. But with four tiles since drawn, our opponent's rack is quite likely to have a biggie now. I found this an extremely difficult position to analyse, so good luck to anyone reading. Ideally we want to leave one or two tiles in the bag, and there certainly are plenty of options. My own inclination here is that two tiles left is better, because there's still plenty of space to play longer moves and there are no really great spots to just dump a single tile. The other factor, I think, is the high probability of our opponent effectively being forced into playing **QI** in the top left corner, and leaving two in the bag punishes it the most.

On the face of it, things look a little bleak if we draw the **Q**, but we could consider ourselves unlucky if we didn't draw something else to go with it. So lets have a run through some possibilities, shall we? **LA(Y)MAN** at M9a for twenty-four, **LA(Y)MEN** at M9a for twenty-four, **(C)AMEL** at L11a for twenty, **MA(C)LE** at L9a for eighteen, **(WO)MAN** at F2d for nineteen, **(Y)EALM** at M11a for twenty, **(C)REAM** at L11a for twenty-four, **(C)LEAR** at L11a for sixteen, **MAR(C)EL** at L8a for twenty-four, **MA(Y)AN** at M9a for twenty-six, **LA(Y)ER** at M9a for eighteen, **M(Y)LAR** at M10a for twenty, **EN(C)ALM** at L9a for twenty, **LAN(C)ER** at L8a for eighteen, **(C)LAME** at L11a for twenty, and **MA(C)ERAL** at M9a for twenty-four.

> **MACLE** *noun, variety of andalusite*
> **YEALM** *verb, prepare straw for thatching*
> **MARCEL** *verb, make a deep soft wave in hair*
> **MAYAN** *adjective, pertaining to maya (illusion)*
> **MYLAR** *noun, strong polyester film*
> **CLAME** *noun, call*
> **MACERAL** *noun, any of the organic units that constitute coal*

And breathe. We're not going to consider emptying the bag, so **MACERAL**'s gone. With our fairly nice rack and the danger of being fenced into a specific **Q** play next go, it's good to have a fairly low-scoring second place to play off, one that doesn't set our opponent up for a big **Q** play if he has it. Also a factor is our opponent was vowel-heavy, so before Komol drew tiles there were at best four vowels out of ten in the bag. So there's no clear indication of vowel or consonant heaviness now.

With an **R** still unseen, that's one tile we can happily get rid of. Despite an **E** generally being better than an **A**, with the **Q** and **J** around, the **A** gives us more ways of playing them off. Having a duplicate of either shouldn't be a big deal. So keeping an **A** is a preferred option over an **E**. With pointy tiles to come, we don't really want to keep an **M**.

I like the score of **MA(Y)AN** and **MAR(C)EL**. **(C)REAM** also scores well. **LA(Y)MAN** and **LA(Y)MEN** score well, but set up the **H** at L12 and leave one in the bag. **(Y)EALM** leaves the double word score at L12 wide open. **(WO)MAN** leaves everything wide open and sets up another **H** spot. I don't want the **R** back with **(C)AMEL/(C)LAME**. **M(Y)LAR** suits the vowelly keep and blocks. So we're down to four.

(C)REAM scores twenty-four and keeps **ALN**. Okay score, leave isn't anything flash with the **LN** combo. The placement of **(C)REAM** opens up quite a few scoring opportunities. It's a decent option overall.

MAR(C)EL scores twenty-six and keeps **AN**. Better score than **CREAM**, don't really want to leave one in the bag here, but it's alright. The play opens up safe scoring plays to the left, which I don't like.

MA(Y)AN scores twenty-six and keeps **ELR**. Don't want the **R** particularly, a bit open to big plays with the **H**, and again opens up the left, but not as much as **MARCEL**.

M(Y)LAR scores twenty and keeps **AEN**. The leave is good, with vowels needed to utilize the double word score by the **C**. We're also better covered against clunky pickups, which are certainly a possibility. It leaves a reasonable, but not game-breaking lane to dump the **Q**, which is what we want.

In the real game, Paul played **(WO)MAN** at F2d. Komol then effectively won the game by hitting him with a big **Q** play – **QUI(C)HE** at L8 for sixty-two.

UNSEEN TILES (1 IN THE BAG):

A₁ E₁ I₁ U₁ D₂ N₁ R₁ T₁

A pre-endgame situation from a game in the 2013 World Scrabble Champions featuring Trevor Hovelmeier versus Piotr Andronowski, who were representing South Africa and Scotland respectively. Piotr to play here, and he's leading by fifty-six. Trevor played **OHO** at A2d the previous move, but we can't really deduce anything from that. Given the pool of unseen tiles, there are bonuses aplenty available.

First off, is it possible to outrun any bonus? Well, the play that combines the best score and least countback is sadly **JEH**(**U**) at M12a for a paltry twenty-six. But this still loses to any bonus on the triple word score (and also to one very neat fit at E14d). So the answer is no. The next thing is to see what bonus words our opponent could potentially hit us with.

> **JEHU** *noun, fast reckless driver*
> **RUINATE** *verb, bring or come to ruin*
> **URANIDE** *noun, radioactive element with an atomic number above 91*
> **TAURINE** *noun, derivative an amino acid obtained from animal bile*

First up, lets have a look at the **F** at A4. There are actually no bonuses possible from the **F**, so no worries there. In column 14 there are a couple that will fit: **UNRATED** at E14d for seventy-three and **RUINATE/URINATE** at D14d. So that's two out of eight. Finally, we come to O1a. **URANIDE(S)**, **URINATE(S)/RUINATE(S)/URANITE(S)/TAURINE(S)**, and **INTRUDE(S)** all fit. So three out of eight. We can't take out both, but the **S** is the biggest threat, so a play onto the **S** will do the trick. Piotr ultimately played **JETE(S)** O4a for twenty-five. This was the best move, too, and it provides a 6 out of 8 or 75 per cent chance of winning. Trevor actually had **URANIDE(S)** ready to go down, so his bonus was blocked in this instance and Piotr got the win.

UNSEEN TILES:

A₁ E₁ E₁ I₁ R₁

This is a fairly linear endgame situation. A pretty blocked board with some room to manoeuvre at the top. There are a couple of **I**s to dump the **Q** onto, but otherwise we want to maximize our score with it and ideally go out in two moves. The top left corner triple word score is open, but our opponent can't use it, so that's heavily to our advantage.

For the best flexibility, you'd be looking to score with the **Q** first and have two places to go out next turn. Lets have a look at our opponent's rack, though. They have **AEEIR**, which actually forms a word: **AERIE** (the nest of a bird of prey). This word plays at C6a, so if we don't cover that, then we won't get a next move.

So the most obvious play here is **QU(A)** B6d for thirty-two. There's one rather big problem with that though: it would merely set up a great out-in-one play for the opponent, with them hooking **QUA** with an **A**, playing **AERIE**, **A(QUA)** at A6a. So what else can we do there? It's hard to play anything parallel at C3a and avoid providing another spot for **AERIE**. There's **KO(A)** and **KE(A)**, which are pretty decent. But the best play here by far is actually to burn our blank: **AQU(A)** at A6d.

It's rather counterintuitive, but there are actually two outs with our remaining rack (**EKNO**) next turn. One is **KENO** (a game of chance) at A1d for thirty, and the other is **O(A)KEN** (made of oak) at A5a for twenty-four. With two options our opponent can't hamper us.

Playthroughs

Now let's have a look at some complete games in detail, move-by-move, from start to finish.

First Playthrough: Nigel Richards v Pakorn Nemitrmansuk, 2009

The first playthrough game is the opening match of the 2009 World Scrabble Championships final between Nigel Richards, originally from New Zealand but often representing Malaysia, and Pakorn Nemitrmansuk of Thailand. Nigel is widely considered to be the best Scrabbler on the planet, and was beginning to put daylight between himself and other top players at this time. Pakorn had lost in two previous WSC finals, so was hoping to make it third time lucky. He had always matched up well against Richards, and was considered by many to be the second-best Scrabbler around. This game was played to Collins Scrabble Words 2007, and I'll point out any noteworthy word list changes which could have affected the play.

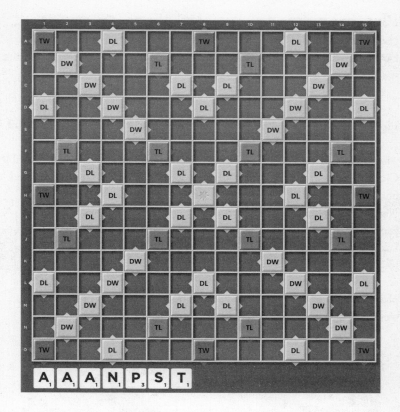

As Nigel finished above Pakorn in the main competition, he went first. Things kicked off with an interesting opening rack. The obvious thing to do here is to play off two **A**s, and a few options do that. **PASTA** (and the similarly themed anagram **TAPAS**) is okay for score, but the score and openness aren't really worth burning the **S** for. The word **PAAN**, a noun meaning a betel leaf, wasn't allowed when this game took place; however, it has the anagram **NAPA** (noun, a soft leather). Another option would be **ATAP** (noun, a palm tree). You could also just play **AA**.

Richards confounded the audience by playing **PA** at G8d for eight points. It is his style to open vertically. In this case, the rack leave of **AANTS** has a certain synergy, but not enough to make it the best option. Analysis favours **NAPA** at H7a for twelve. The advantage of this placement is it creates an **S** hook lane in a fruitful position without giving much scoring potential away. The **P** in the third position makes parallel plays a little more awkward than **ATAP**. But the differences are fairly marginal.

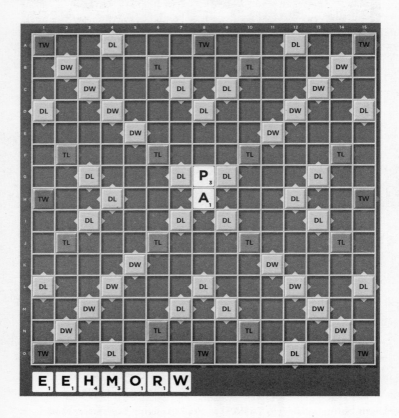

Always look for a bonus first. Nigel's move implies he has something close to a bonus. Most of the time, Richards would also be keeping an **A** back and simply choose to play off whichever vowel balanced his rack.

If you're struggling to see the bonus here, think about prefixes and suffixes. Then look for possible subwords that could combine to form a longer word. Note this rack combines with **B** and **V** to make eight-letter words. Pakorn quickly put down **HOMEW(A)RE** at H3a for sixty-seven points. The rack goes with **B** to make **HOME(B)REW** and **V** to make **WHOME(V)ER**.

(-58) <u>NIGEL</u> 8–67 PAKORN

Richards is almost spoilt for choice. There are no less than eight different bonus words here: some obscure but highly useful Scrabble favourites, as well as a few common words. However, there is just the one seven letter bonus here: **ISTANAS** (*istana*, noun, [Malay] a royal palace). Pluralizing **HOMEWARE** would net a good score, but there's one run-of-the-mill word through the **M** that tops even that.

Other bonus plays are **S(H)AITANS** through the **H**, **(M)ANTISSA** and **SATANIS(M)** through the **M**, **(E)NTASIAS** through the **E**, and finally **A(R)TISANS** and **TSA(R)INAS** through the somewhat obscured **R**.

Nigel spots the double-double **STA(M)INAS** at E5d for ninety points.

NIGEL 98–67 PAKORN (-31)

Unfortunately no floating **C** for **AIRBRI(C)K**, so no third bonus just yet. Lots of moderate options, but no real standout play. The priority is to get rid of an **I** and an **R**, whilst it would be nice to dump the **B** too.

A few of the outlandish words available are **KARRI** (noun, a type of Australian gum tree), **KIRRI** (noun, a stick), and one that wasn't allowed back then, **BRIKI** (noun, a small metal pot used for preparing coffee).

BIRK (noun, a birch tree) at K4d for twenty-eight creates a nice **S** hook lane, but there's already one of those on the board (**HOMEWARE-S**), and there are only two **S**s unseen. **BRI(N)K** at J2a for twenty-seven through the

N is a solid option. There's also **BIRK(S)** and **BRIK(S)** (*brik*, noun, a Tunisian filled pastry), both at L1a for twenty-eight. **BIRK(S)** allows far fewer scoring plays in the 2 column than **BRIK(S)**, and that's ultimately what Pakorn goes for.

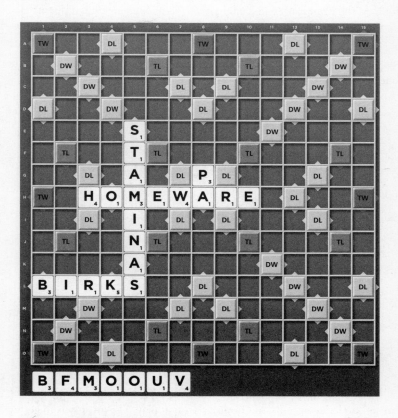

(+3) NIGEL 98–95 PAKORN

An ugly rack for Nigel. I think most people sitting with this rack would be eying up **OVUM** (an egg cell, plural **OVA**). The **B** in the bottom left corner looks inviting for (**B**)**UMF** (noun, paperwork) or (**B**)**UFO** (noun, a black tincture). **BUMF** scores thirty-three leaving **VOOB**. **BUFO** scores twenty-seven leaving a less horrific **BMOV**. Either way, you're almost resigned to playing off some rubbish next turn. The **M** creates a bit more scoring potential and has synergy with the **B**. (**B**)OMB for thirty would mean a ghastly **UV** combination.

Nigel opted for none of these. He picked **BO(E)UF** at F10d for twenty-four. As the word is used in combination (*boeuf bourguignon*), it doesn't take an **S** hook. This move has a few defensive merits, taking out the **R** and **E** floaters in **HOMEWARE** and restricting the first **S** in **STAMINAS**. As his rack is poor, it is to his benefit to keep things tight whilst he balances his tiles out. I think (**B**)UMF at L1d for thirty-three is just as good, though.

NIGEL 122–95 PAKORN (-27)

A powerful pickup of **COTZ** for Pakorn. With a balanced rack and a number of premium squares available, there are a lot of options. The main focus is the bottom left corner, looking for any big **Z** triple letter and double word score combination, or some sort of play using the **B** in **BIRKS** which also uses the **Z** and hits the triple word score. Unfortunately neither exist.

I think most top players would see **ZO(I)C** (pertaining to animals) at J2d for thirty-five and be satisfied. This is a very strong play: good score and a relatively bonus-friendly leave of **AIRT**. There are, however, some devilish setups for the **Z**. **(F)RIT** at J10 for seven points sets up a potentially massive **FRIT-Z** hook, but that's too obvious because you can score eighteen points with the same letters off the **B** (with **(B)RIT**), and given that, it would be typically easy to take out. The latter setup would take a genius to spot and play, given there are so many solid options elsewhere. **OCT(A)** (noun, a unit of cloud cover) at G2a for twenty-one creates a lovely hotspot in an otherwise quiet looking part of the board. **ACT(A)** in the same place does the same job, but the **A** is nicer to keep back.

The beauty of **OCT(A)** is that if the area around the play is left alone by your opponent, then you are guaranteed to have a seventy points move next turn: **ZA** at F2a. The play would arouse suspicion at the top level, and it creates a place that's easy to block and, often, score relatively well at the same time. There is, however, a backup plan. Picking up one of the ten unseen **E**s will mean **ZA(I)RE** (noun, a monetary unit) plays from J2d for sixty-eight.

Strategically, then, **OCT(A)** has a massive upside, but it's very difficult to weigh up against **ZO(I)C**, which scores fourteen points more. Computer analysis has them about level, but I suspect a human opponent would take out the hotspot at F2 more often than a machine. Pakorn confounded everyone by playing **AZOTIC** (containing nitrogen) at J11d for thirty-nine. It scores well and keeps the useful **R**. However, it creates lots of high-scoring openings, and many of these pointy replies would also close off that part of the board, leaving a net benefit to Nigel.

Inference from Nigel's move of **BO(E)UF** suggests he wasn't holding anything brilliant, but with four tiles to come, his new rack could be pretty much anything. **AZOTIC** is a bit of a Hail Mary play, one that you'd typically reserve for when you're miles behind. Alternatively, if there is a massive opening elsewhere which you can't really do much with, then creating a second big hotspot like this means both players typically get hefty scores.

(-12) NIGEL 122–134 PAKORN

Again, plenty of choices here. Nigel has a number of common words available that score nicely. His focus will be around **AZOTIC**. He can fit **DOME** at J12d for forty-two, leaving a somewhat clunky **COV**. **V(I)DEO** goes neatly through the **I** for thirty-four points at N10a. That takes out a dangerous opening and keeps back **COM**, pretty much guaranteeing a decent play alongside the **Z** if it's untouched next go.

Elsewhere **VO(I)CE** or **VO(I)CED** play for thirty-six and forty respectively at J2d. Whilst it's nice to leave the hook back, **VOICER** is too easy for the opponent to make, and there isn't much potential to score with the **D** hook anyway without a bonus. The four points differential is also a factor. **VO(I)**

CED leaves **MO**, which again has potential for parallel plays alongside **AZOTIC**.

Ideally you'd want to play **V(I)DEO** because it takes out a lot of easy scoring options, but the score and leave of **VO(I)CED** edge it, and Nigel opted for it too.

NIGEL 162–134 PAKORN (-28)

Not much to think about this time. In other situations, you would like to dump the **J** off for a nice 30–40 points and see if the rack can mature into a bonus. But with forty-eight points on offer, as well as taking out the biggest scoring threat, this is a no-brainer. **DREN(C)H** goes down at O7a, the best play by a distance.

(-20) NIGEL 162–182 PAKORN

The best fifteen or so plays all involve words in column 12. Lots of straightforward three-letter words from J12d rate highly here, particularly ones using one of the duplicate **R**s. A nice spot is the six-letter word **MORTAR**, which slots in from G12d for thirty-nine. Usually in this sort of situation, you'd be concerned about leaving a bonus lane in column 13. However, whatever you play here there will be a lane available. The two **Y**s unseen make the G13 spot (making **MY**) a little bit more of an issue.

GRAM and **TRAM** at I12d are strong options, but the best of the bunch is **GROMA** in the same place for forty-three. It scores better than the alternatives, and the leave of **RT** has a little bit of synergy. **GROMA** is a Roman surveying instrument.

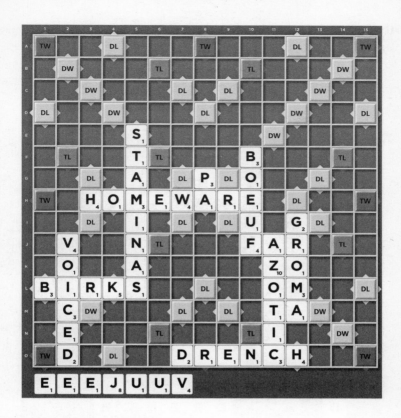

NIGEL 205–182 PAKORN (-23)

An awful pickup of **EEUUV**. With such a dismal rack, there aren't many possible words. Fortunately, they all play somewhere. The two main dumps here are **JEU** (a game, plural **JEUX**) and **JUVE** (noun, a juvenile). Others are possible, but they don't get rid of a **U**. A second **U** is far worse than a second **E**, particularly if the **V** is still sitting on your rack.

JUVE plays in columns 4 and 11, whilst **JEU** plays in column 11 and row N. The difference between the leaves **EEU** and **EEUV** is difficult to call. I think a lot of people would think the **V** improves the leave, due to the vowel heaviness, but actually the negative synergy with the **U** and the fact that **V** is a poor tile anyway mean that the **V** makes things slightly worse, if anything.

I like keeping things tight here, whilst waiting for the rack to improve.

JUVE at C11d for thirty-two also scores a bit more, and I rate this as the best play. Pakorn's choice of **JEU** at N6a, thirty-one points is pretty good too, though.

(-8) <u>NIGEL 205</u>–213 PAKORN

Nigel picks up an **S** and has a rack of some potential. Note here that **OMA** (German word for a grandmother) was added six years after this final took place, so isn't available; otherwise it would be very handy here. It is tempting to look around at moves that play two or three consonants off here, but there aren't many places to bonus, and it sacrifices a lot of score when simple plays for 35–40 points are available on a pretty tight board.

A vast number of options pluralize **HOMEWARE**. A few four-letter words go, but the five-letter words are better, scoring just that bit more and helping balance the rack with one less consonant. **TRAPS** at D11d for thirty-nine is good, but **DRAPS** or **PRADS** at the same spot are slightly better. Whilst **DRAPS** scores one more point than **PRADS**, it also provides a better floater for our opponent to bonus through. So there isn't much between them. Equally sound is Nigel's play of **LAST** at J13d for thirty-eight. It keeps **DPR** back which has a bit of synergy, scoring potential, and, if it matures into a bonus next go, would probably slot in nicely from A11 with an -**ER** or -**ED** ending.

NIGEL 243–213 PAKORN (-30)

Not a bad pickup this time for Pakorn. He'll be making a mental note of the **E** hook on **FARL**, (both **FARL** and **FARLE** mean an oatmeal cake) – another position with a few steady options and a number of lanes to choose from.

If you wanted to be crafty, and you knew the word **VENDUE** (noun, public sale), then you would play **ENDUE** at B4d for sixteen points and set up the **V** hook. You could also simply play **VENDUE** in the same place and score thirty-two, which is less fun, but better in my opinion. **VENDEE** (noun, buyer) plays in a few spots, but leaves you with the **U**. The regulation play is **VENUE** at A4d for twenty-six, keeping a solid **DE** back whilst opening things up a bit. But with the **FARLE** hook, it also plays at F14d for a couple of points more, if you fancy a bit more of a gamble. Pakorn plays **VENUE** in the top left corner.

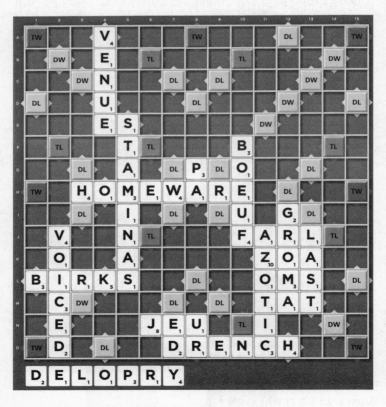

(+4) NIGEL 243–239 PAKORN

One of those situations where finding a bonus is one thing, but being certain enough to play it is quite another. So what you do think? **DEPLOYER** or **REDEPLOY**? Well, they're both valid. **DEPLOYER** plays in one spot, but only scores sixty-eight and opens up one big scoring opportunity. **REDEPLOY** plays from either column 1 or column 3. The first position scores eighty-two and the other seventy-four.

Usually that sort of scoring differential makes it a no-brainer. But playing in the first column creates two huge opportunities. This isn't great when you're eighty-six points ahead. A triple-triple is a real threat in this situation because it will instantly put you a bonus or more behind. There are two blanks unseen and the **R** in the second place is pretty helpful. Then there's the **Y** below a triple word score. Computer analysis shows your opponent will use that on two thirds of replies, scoring on average fifty-five points. Ouch. Most bonuses play and most clunk racks will do heavy damage. Placing **REDEPLOY** further along makes it far harder to score and bonus. Even then a bonus reply would often leave a lane for one of your own, and there'd also typically be more floating tiles to work with. Nigel selects the best spot, B3a.

NIGEL 317–239 PAKORN (-78)

A blow to Pakorn's chances, but on the plus side Nigel's bonus didn't burn any blanks, so there are still two left to help mount a comeback. With twenty-nine tiles left unseen, there are still five **I**s to come, so it becomes a priority to play one off here. The main play to consider here is **FOETID**, and where you place it. C9a scores one point more than A10a.

So how would you decide between the two? Well, the one obvious spot for a bonus play is to hook **FARL**. Playing at C9a badly obscures this opportunity. It also doesn't really create much in return. It's more of a blocking play, as **FOETID** doesn't take a hook itself. The A10a spot provides floaters to play down from, as well as leaving the **FARL** hook open. But there is one other possibility here: a lovely overlap from the **V** – (**V**)ETOED at A4a for forty-eight points, and that tops **FOETID**. Well done if you spotted this. Pakorn plays **FOETID** from A10a.

(+37) <u>NIGEL 317</u>–280 PAKORN

A fragile lead for Nigel, with two blanks unseen. Two **G**s, three **N**s, and three **I**s are also left to come, so the extension of **DRENCH** to **DRENCHING** seems almost inevitable. With sixteen tiles in the bag, Nigel is not far from the finishing post, and he's got some good scoring potential to try and outrun his opponent.

QUAIS (*quai*, noun, quay) is the clear play here. Nigel would dearly love to play from F14 down, hooking **FARL** and shutting that space down. But there's one big problem: an **-ING** ending would play parallel to the **Q**, **U**, and **A**, and the remaining tiles scream **-ING** bonus. Nigel can score heavily from D11d, with the added advantage of setting up an **I** spot with which he can score next turn if Pakorn bonuses, meaning he should still hold the edge. **RICHARDS** plays **QUAIS** at D11d for fifty-one points to go eighty-eight in front.

NIGEL 368–280 PAKORN (-88)

Pakorn finally hits one of the blanks and has a ton of bonus plays available. Given the scoreline, it would be tempting to take the forty-eight points from **DRENCH-ING**, opening up another lane in the bottom right corner, and have a chance to hit a bonus play next turn, hopefully taking the lead. Whilst it looks impossible to block bonuses playing in the last two columns, a move utilizing the **FARL** hook – either **FARLE** or **FARLS** using a blank played in column 14 – could potentially block all of those possibilities. Alternatively, Nigel will score well in column 12 using the **Q-I** spot, wipe out most or all of the forty-eight points gained, and leave around four tiles in the bag, at which point it will be very difficult to get a bonus and draw something strong enough to win.

So that leaves the biggest bonuses available, **(D)EVELING** and **(D)ELETING**, both at A15d for eighty points. They would leave Pakorn six points down, with Nigel still to play and at worst getting a nice score alongside the **Q**. So it is to Pakorn's advantage that the bonus plays create volatility, by setting up a big **X** spot at F14, because he's still a big underdog. Pakorn opts for **DELETING**.

(+8) <u>NIGEL 368</u>–360 PAKORN

UNSEEN TILES (4 IN THE BAG):

A₁ E₁ I₁I₁ G₂ N₁N₁ T₁ W₄ X₈ ☐

Not only has the lead been almost wiped out, but Pakorn's last play used the **D** for **(D)ILATORY**, which would have netted eighty-nine points. The **-ING** is still out there to extend **DRENCH**, there's a blank left, and the bonus has created a damaging spot for the **X**, with plenty of big plays from A8d like **I(L)EX** possible. Nigel can score well and has a small lead, but this is anyone's game.

With four in the bag there are two ways to go: either to try and play off as many tiles as possible, or leave one or two to make it harder for Pakorn, who is also very low on time. If your own clock were running out, you might try and shorten the game by going for the higher turnover play. There's only really one that is worth considering: **(T)ARTILY** at A13d for twenty-eight points. This takes out the easiest **X** spot at F14 and also alters the **Q** spot in lane 12, limiting the potential, although **ANI** at D12d would still slot in. Having five on the rack makes it hard to go out in one, but it's a solid choice without ever realistically being the best option. There are a number of moves that leave one in the bag. With so much firepower unseen, this is certainly better than leaving two behind. **ITA** at D12d for thirty-five looks pretty good, leaving **LORY** and almost guaranteeing another decent score next play (such as on one of the triple word scores or using the **Y** spot at J6). With the **Q-I** spot open, keeping an **I** back is important if playing elsewhere, so that counts against **I(D)LY** at O1a for thirty-six. But **A(D)RY** is also available in the same place and is a superior option. The highest-scoring play available is **AIRY** at C12d for forty-six points. It increases the lead to fifty-four, but also empties the bag. On most boards that would be sufficient to clinch the game, but with two big scoring spots and a couple of triple word scores open, then it's not so straight-forward. It also makes it easier for Pakorn to quickly work out and play an optimal sequence. Computer analysis suggests **AIRY** is the best move, but doesn't account for the time factor. Nigel goes with **A(D)RY** at O1a for thirty-six.

NIGEL 404–360 PAKORN (-44)

UNSEEN TILES (1 IN THE BAG):

A E I I L O T T

Almost spoilt for choice here. Forty-four points down, but more than enough ammunition for Pakorn to win the game. But he's desperately low on time. Can he find the move that wins no matter which tile he draws from the bag? What would you do? Cash in the **X**? Extend **DRENCH** with the **-ING**? What about that **Q-I** spot, the main scoring spot for Nigel?

This position is very tough to work through, even if you had a good ten minutes to go through all of the permutations. My first instinct here would be to play **WEX** or **WAX** at D14d for fifty-eight, leaving **GINN**. You then have **DRENCH-ING** for forty-eight or **GINN** at C12d for thirty-nine to play next turn, regardless of your pickup. That intuitively feels like it could withstand anything, but it actually loses if one of the two **I**s is in the bag. See if you can work out the winning combo for your opponent with **AEILOTT**, scoring an aggregate of fifty-nine points, winning by a single point on countback.

So, **WEX** or **WAX** is a good start, winning three quarters of the time. What about playing **DRENCHING** first? Well, it is easy to block the big **X** spot. With the unseen tiles, words like **ILEA** and **TELIA** slot nicely into column 14, leaving plenty of flexibility to use the **Q-I** spot. At M7a, we had **WOX** as a backup play, but this leaves us losing to a good out-in-two. A consonant pickup looks bad for us holding **NWX?**, and indeed drawing either **T** means defeat.

The **L**, however, is, okay because it means neither **ILEA** (plural of **ILEUM**, a part of the small intestine) or **TELIA** (plural of **TELIUM**, a structure produced by rust fungi) are available for the opponent. But drawing the **O** also loses (**FLOX**, crucially wasn't allowed at the time). **ILEA** wins to the two best responses of **WOX** at M7a, or optimally **XI** at C12d, with **TIT** at C12d or **TIT(E)** at E6d respectively. So playing **DRENCHING** only triumphs five out of eight times with perfect endgame play.

The move that would theoretically win regardless of what's in the bag is **WING** at C12d for forty-six. The advantages of this play are that it forces the opponent to block the X spot and ensures they will score poorly over two turns, since the **Q-I** spot is taken. The **A**, **E**, and **I** still give a fifty-four point play from A8d. The **O** means you have a high-scoring outplay next turn (**X(E)NON** at G6d). Cheap **X** plays using C9 are enough to scrape a win with the more awkward draws.

Did you find the fifty-nine point play sequence earlier? It was **TIT** at C12d for thirty, followed by **LOA(V)E** (verb, form a head or loaf) or **LAE(V)O** (adjective, turning to the left) for twenty-nine at A1a. Pakorn played (**DRENCH)ING** at O7a for forty-eight points with only one second left on his clock. Will it cost him the opening game of the 2009 World Scrabble Championship final?

(-4) NIGEL 404–408 PAKORN

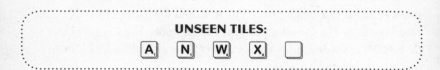

UNSEEN TILES:

A, N, W, X, □

The last tile in the bag is an **A**! Surely Nigel can't win now. Pakorn can play the simple **WAXIN(G)** at J15d for twenty-four, or he can drag things out with **WAX** for sixty at D14d. There's also **F(L)AX** at A8d for fifty-four points. Is there any possible way of manufacturing a win, even after Pakorn's probable time penalties? Whatever Richards plays, he will lose by plenty to anything but a horrible mistake. The most Nigel can possibly score is **O(L)LIE** (noun, a jump in skateboarding) at A8d and **TIT** at C14d. That forty-eight points is dwarfed by the sixty for **WAX**. Blocking **WAX** doesn't score enough to win after time penalties and **WAXIN**(**G**).

My thoughts watching this live were that the only realistic way to triumph was to score with **TIT** or **LIT** at C14d for thirty and go twenty-six up, then hope Pakorn panics, mistracks, or assumes (with no time to check) that there's a big follow-up play to come. He may not even take in the scoreline and the thirty points just scored. Then you still have to pray that Pakorn throws down **WAXIN**(**G**) for twenty-four and goes over on time, thus losing by four points. I suppose a more underhand option would be to play some ridiculous phoney and hope it goes unnoticed, such as pretending to play **TOE** at A6 then sneakily drop another letter down for **TOEL**(**FOETID**)*. Nigel played **O(L)LIE** at A8d for eighteen.

NIGEL 422–408 PAKORN (-14)

Even the threat of **TIT** at C12d for thirty isn't a problem now. **WAX** at D14d scores sixty, but you lose thirty points from **TIT** and a further two points on countback with the **N** on your rack. So that's a net twenty-eight points. **WAXIN**(**G**) at J15d for twenty-four gains six points (**ITT**) on countback, so that's a net thirty points. Pakorn goes over on time, but plays the best move **WAXIN**(**G**) and wins the game 425–419. He went on to win the final 3–1 and was crowned 2009 World Scrabble Champion.

Second Playthrough: Komol Panyasoponlert v Craig Beevers

The other game is from the 2013 World Scrabble Championships, featuring runner-up Komol Panyasoponlert and, err, me, who came fifth.

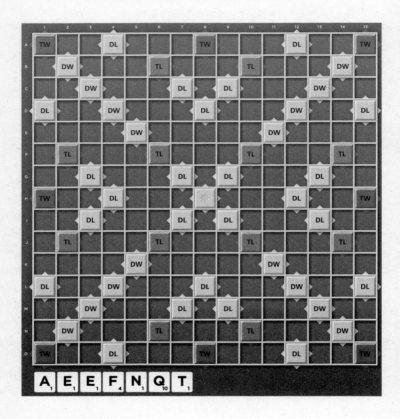

KOMOL 0–0 CRAIG

Not too much to think about here for the young Thai player. There's only one **Q** word available and it scores more than anything else. The H7a position is best because it doesn't leave the **A** adjacent to a double letter score.

The next highest scoring move is **NEAFE**, a word meaning fist. But the actual second-best play after **QAT** is to exchange **EFQ**. Komol plays **QAT** at H7a for twenty-four.

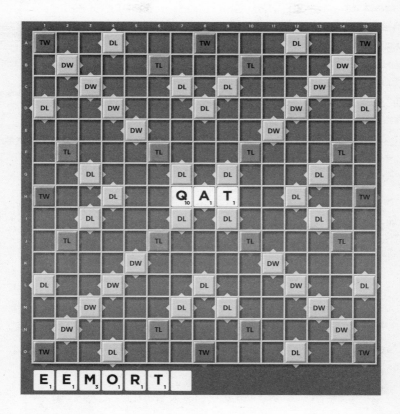

KOMOL 24–0 CRAIG (-24)

A nice rack to open up with. The highest theoretical score is an eight-letter word starting or ending in **A** with the **M** on a double letter score. There are three eights possible, using the blank as a **D**, **S**, or **V**, but none of them fit the criteria. Those words are **MODERATE**, **EROTEMAS**, and **OVERTAME** (**EROTEMA** being a rhetorical question and **OVERTAME** being an adjective).

There are no sevens using the blank as **I**, so that rules out a defensive play underlapping the whole of **QAT**. So next option is the blank as an **S**. There are three bonuses, two common words, and the somewhat unlikely **EMOTERS** (noun, one who shows exaggerated emotion). Of the other two, **METEORS** hits the triple letter score with the **M**, whilst **REMOTES** does not. I played **METEORS** at B10d for seventy-eight.

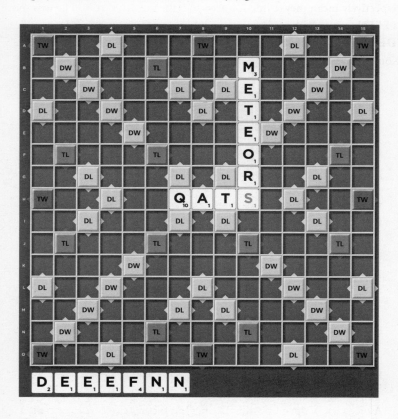

(-54) <u>KOMOL 24–78 CRAIG</u>

Some duplicates to sort out, but nothing too problematic. The main scoring line revolves around playing parallel to the right of **METEORS**. It is tempting to concentrate too much on placing the **F** on the double word score and work from there. Indeed there is one strong move that does this, **NEF** (noun, an ornamental table stand for cutlery) at C12d for twenty-six, and many players would be satisfied at seeing this and put it down.

NEF ticks the box of playing off duplicates; although it still leaves two **E**s, a leave of **DEEN** is decent enough. Higher scoring options are available from C12d, such as **FEED** and **FEND**, but the leaves of **ENN** and **EEN** respectively mean they're inferior plays, despite the extra score. The best move is **FEEN** (noun, Irish word for man), playing at C10d and C12d. The leave (**DEN**) and score are superior to **NEF**, as well as being a bit better defensively. Komol plays **FEEN** at C12d for twenty-seven.

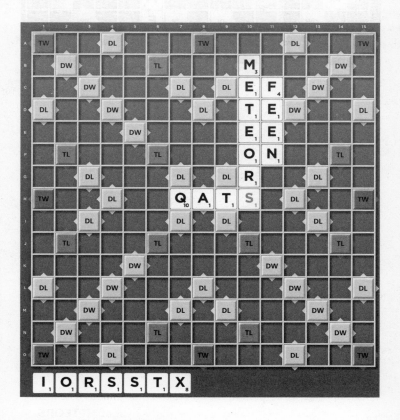

KOMOL 51–78 CRAIG (+27)

A bonus-friendly rack, spoilt somewhat by the **X** tile. There are no sevens or eights possible, so it comes down to dumping the **X** for the best balance of score and leave. There are a couple of options here: below **QATS** using the **I** (so **TIX** or **SIX** at I6a for thirty-two), or extend **TE** in row D.

Firstly, lets look at **TIX** (plural noun meaning tickets) v **SIX**. The main deciding factor here is the leave. Dumping the extra **S** and keeping **ORST** provides something stronger than **ORSS**. So **SIX** is better. What about **TE**? That extends to (**TE**)**X** (a unit of density for yarn), (**TE**)**XT**, or even (**TE**)**XTS**. Again, the **T** goes well with the other letters, and the availability of the hooks provides a bonus lane. So simply playing (**TE**)**X** at D10a for twenty is pretty good. I don't think there's much between (**TE**)**X** and **SIX**, and which one you go for would probably depend on your style. I opted for **SIX** at I6a for thirty-two.

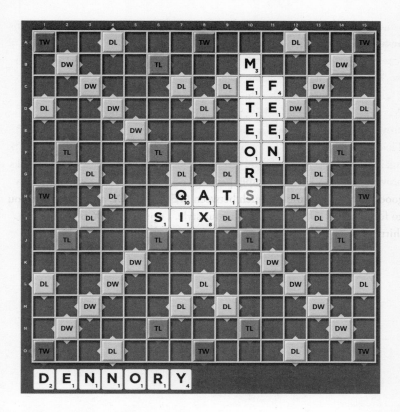

(-59) <u>KOMOL</u> 51–110 CRAIG

A somewhat middling rack, with **QI** providing an obvious lane to sort out the duplicate **N**. The thinking for this move is about finding the word that fits and scores the most. The fact that only one letter on the rack can go below **S**, **QI**, and **AX** should help to narrow things down quite quickly. So you're basically looking for a word with **ONE** in it, or ending in **ON** or starting with **NE**.

There are a surprisingly vast number of options. **DONER**, **DRONE**, **DONE**, **NONE**, **ONER**, **RONE**, and of course **ONE** all contain **ONE**. Without the **E** there is **YON**, leaving a strong **DENR** – the best of that particular bunch. Starting with **NE** includes **NERDY**. But there was one other **ONE** word I omitted: the less common spelling of 'ornery' is **ONERY**, which Komol puts down at J6a for forty-four – the standout play and an awkward word to see.

KOMOL 95–110 CRAIG (+15)

The extra volatility did not go my way this time, picking out a dreadful **UV** combination. The tendency would be to try and look for a floating letter that allows you to dump the **UV** off. **VU(M)** is possible here at the top, but only scores face value. In most situations the best plays won't allow you to drop both awkward letters. Here, however, there's quite a good option of **VROUS** at K3a for thirty-two. **VROU**, **VROW**, and **VROUW** come up an awful lot and are Afrikaans words for woman or wife.

Given the score and the way the board was shaping up, I didn't want to open things up. The **S** was good for controlling the board whilst I maintained a small lead, and could help me to capitalize when my opponent tried to create some opportunities. I opted for **VO(TE)R** at D8a for twenty-four. It leaves **HSTU** (splitting up the **UV** combination), blocks some scoring lines, and makes having an **S** more important for getting a bonus word down.

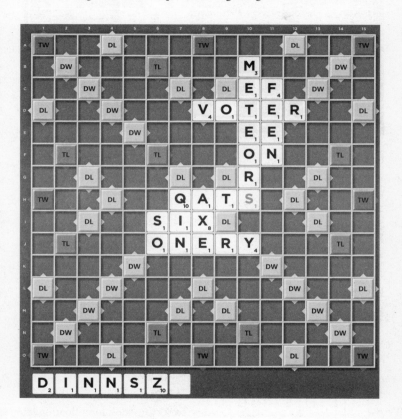

(-39) <u>KOMOL</u> 95–134 CRAIG

A powerful draw for Komol. No bonus yet, but with this sort of rack you'd think a good score followed by a bonus is on the cards. Ideally, you would want to keep the **S**, but it looks the only way to score here.

Although **D(O)N** at C9d isn't bad, **ZIN** or **ZINS** at K4a are the main options. Many players would worry about using the **Z** here, or indeed the placement of the **Z** one square above a double word score. The location isn't a big issue; while it will upgrade a lot of opponent's plays (particularly vowel dumps) to greater scores, those plays in turn will generally create hotspots as well. Playing the **S** gains an extra fifteen points, so that has to be the right option. Komol plays **ZINS** for forty-two.

KOMOL 137–134 CRAIG (-3)

Another ugly combination: a pair of Us. This is one occasion where I think everyone would spot the best move. **(Z)ULU** at K4d sticks out like a sore thumb. There is only one other **S** to come, so leaving the **S** off is a good thing strategically. The four points gained by **(Z)ULUS** isn't enough to offset the leave. Whilst **HMST** is consonant-heavy, it only takes one vowel to get a good forty or more points, hooking **ZULU** next turn.

There is a risk of being vowelless, but Scrabble is a game of risk and reward, with very little black and white. I played **(Z)ULU** at K4d for twenty-six and crossed my fingers...

(-23) <u>KOMOL 137</u>–160 CRAIG

Another less than ideal pickup. On a different board, the available bonus players would be a lot easier to find. There are three seven-letter words: **DUNNITE**, **DUNTING**, and **TUNDING**. None of those will go down here. Lots of eights possible with **A**s and **E**s.

Unfortunately, Komol only has a **U** and an **L** to work with. There is only one very clunky-sounding bonus word that plays: **UNUNITED**. It is worth seventy at N2a and sixty at N4a. If you didn't fancy risking that, the next best play again utilizes the **O** in **VOTER** at the top. **UD(O)N** at B9 is a lovely move and ranks right up there with **UNUNITED** in the better position, due to the strength of the leave and the strategic deficit in providing such a juicy triple word spot for comeback plays at O8. Komol plays **UN(U)NITED** at N2a for seventy.

KOMOL 207–160 CRAIG (-47)

Lots of scoring letters to hit back with here. Whilst there are moderate scores to be had adding an **S** to **ZULU,** this is really all about the central triple word score at the bottom. Parallel plays offer the highest scores: **MESH**, **HEMS**, **HEHS**, the two best are **METHS** and **HETHS**. There with the last two **S**s sitting on the rack, there is a little more value in keeping both of them behind and just playing **METH** or **HETH**. Leaving an **S** sticking out meaning a lot of bonuses would play from H12d onto it. **S**s are particularly useful on this tight board. At the time I wasn't sure of **HETH(S)**, which is a Hebrew letter, and played safe with **METHS** O8a for forty-five, knowing the loss of six points was offset a little by the better leave.

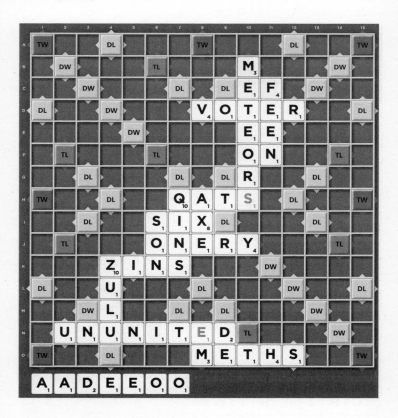

(+2) <u>KOMOL 207</u>–205 CRAIG

Not the sort of pickup you want after a bonus. The are only really two places to look at here: the **L** in **ZULU** at M4 and the **V** in **VOTER** at D8. There are a lot of possibilities with the **L**. **A(L)OO**, meaning potato, slots in nicely. There's **O(L)EA**, the plural of **OLEUM**, meaning oil, and **O(L)EO**, meaning margarine. Onto the **V** there's only **DEE(V)** (an evil spirit) and **DEA(V)E** (to deafen).

DEAVE scores the best of any with twenty-seven, but leaves an ugly **AOO**, whilst the **L** plays all register sixteen points. My personal favourite is **A(L)OO**, which keeps back a decent **ADEE**, meaning **DEA(V)E** will be playable next turn if the **V** is untouched. However, that makes it easier for plays from O1a to fit in, as **AN** has more back hooks than **ON**. Computer analysis likes playing **DEA(V)E** straight away. Komol opted for **O(L)EA** at M3a for sixteen.

KOMOL 223–<u>205 CRAIG</u> (-18)

Another scoring rack. Can't do anything useful with the **ZULU-S** spot.

There's **CHI(V)** (a verb meaning to stab) onto the **V**, which scores relatively highly, but sets up an easy **E** hook, and with the opponent just playing off three vowels including an **E**, you don't want to give them a scoring opportunity which they'll very likely have access to. In terms of score and leave, **WHIC(H)** at K11d for thirty-two is the star. Keeping back **RST** is very powerful. At the time I was preoccupied with giving nothing away and blocking the **S**. **WHIC(H)** provides a reasonable scoring spot for a vowel dump. There are a some decent options at C9d, the likes of **R(O)W**, **T(O)W**, and **R(O)WT**, holding back a powerful combination. Ultimately, I think all these mentioned moves are better than what I picked, which was **CRWT(H)** at K11d for twenty-six. One of those classic Scrabble words, 'crwth' originates from Welsh and is an archaic stringed instrument.

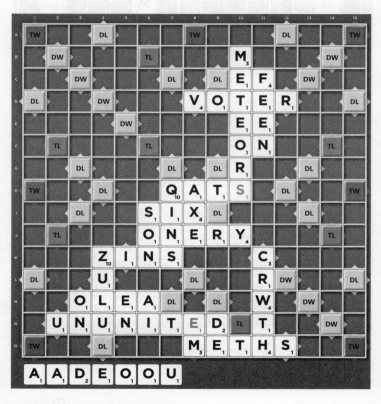

(-8) KOMOL 223–231 CRAIG

Whilst I was mainly playing off consonants, Komol was getting more vowelly rubbish. It is just about worth playing a move here, ahead of exchanging. **(W)OOED** at M11a for eighteen looks tolerable on the face of it, but there are still five **A**s unseen, so holding back **AAU** is asking for trouble. It also creates great lanes for bonusing or scoring whilst we cross fingers picking four tiles out of the bag.

U(R)AO (a mineral), **AU(R)A**, and **AU(R)AE** in row L aren't too bad. But the clear best play is **DOU(R)A**, meaning a cereal grain, at L8a for sixteen. It keeps back **AEO** and doesn't give much away, which is generally a good thing with that sort of leave. Komol plays **DOURA**.

KOMOL 239–231 CRAIG (-8)

Well, some more vowels arrived, but not the prettiest rack to deal with. Still no reasonable play in the bottom left corner of the board. **DOURA** does, however, take an H, which opens up a lot of possibilities. Ideally you'd look to play off the **V** and at least a couple of vowels, but there are no decent options, with **VI(V)A/VI(V)O** scoring next to nothing.

A slightly different option is **(W)HIO** (a New Zealand blue duck), at M12a for twenty-five. This takes an **S**, so this would create a more productive place for it, but it also allows the **S** spot to be shut down quite easily. **OHIA** (a Hawaiian evergreen tree) at K13d for twenty-four looks nice, but makes the bonus lane available to plays not using an **S**. So that leaves **HOI** at L13d twenty-two, which is sound strategically with a reasonable score and leave. I plumped for **HOI** in the end.

(-14) <u>KOMOL</u> 239–253 CRAIG

Finally a good pickup for Komol. This is one of those positions where you either know the word or you don't. If you don't, then you're dropping a good 20–30 points in terms of score and leave. **JAR(V)EY** at A8d for fifty-seven is the standout play. **JARVEY** is an informal, obsolete word for the driver of a horse-drawn taxi.

If you don't know the word, then the next best choice is **J(EF)E**, a word for a chief, at C9a for forty-one points, leaving a fairly dismal **AAORY**. The next best plays after that drop off even further. This is one occasion where wisdom and strategy are no substitute for word knowledge. Komol has all of those qualities and played **JAR(V)EY** for fifty-seven.

KOMOL 296–253 CRAIG (-43)

A body blow, hit by a fifty-seven point play on a tight board. It also stopped me playing something like **VAL(V)E** through that **V**. There are a couple of good scores still available, but being so close to a bonus, with an almost unblockable lane and a forty-three point deficit, then there's no real advantage to burning the good tiles unless it scores really big.

So a move like **APES** from M1a for forty-three just isn't worth it. It only pulls me level and leaves a pretty rubbish **ILV**. The board has been shaped to make the **S** a massive tile. So what about bonus-friendly leaves? Ideally, you'd look to dump the **V** plus a vowel. This is doable, but frustrating, because the best options block useful floaters. Moves like **IV(Y)** at F6a for eleven. I opted for extra score with **VI(A)** at B6a for fourteen. This looks to be the best option, along with the rather cute **P(R)I(EF)** (a proof) at C7a.

(+29) <u>**KOMOL 296–267 CRAIG**</u>

UNSEEN TILES   (21 IN THE BAG):

A A A A E E E E I I
I I O B B D F G G G
L L L P R S T W

A really tricky situation. All of the recent plays suggest a big move is coming sooner or later. There are two approaches. One is to gamble and go for a move that allows to you block column 14 next time, but makes any immediate bonus that much more fatal. The other is to try and create ways to score elsewhere and potentially outrun a bonus, knowing you may get a good counterplay to anything in column 14 with all those triple word scores open.

Going for the block-in-two route means playing something like **DOP** at M13d and then hooking it next turn. Risky, and could open up big non-bonus plays too. There are a lot of **A**s, **B**s, and **L**s left, so perhaps by playing onto the **E** or **Y** in **JARVEY** you may end blocking a bonus there, such as ones ending in -**LY**, -**ABLE**, etc. The best play I think is the pretty simple **KA(Y)** at F6a for twenty, setting up **O-KAY** next turn, with only one other **O** out there. But there are loads of options. Komol goes for **PAND(Y)** (to punish by striking the hand) at F4a for thirteen, leaving a powerful **CKO** to counter a column 14 bonus with, or to score at E5.

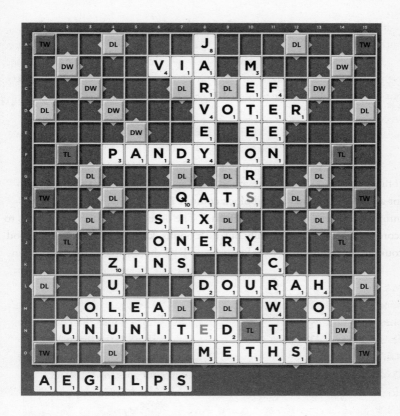

KOMOL 309–<u>267 CRAIG</u> (-42)

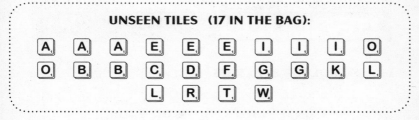

UNSEEN TILES (17 IN THE BAG):

A A A E E E I I I O
O B B C D F G G K L
L R T W

Great pick up. I'd been staring at **PAIGLES** ('paigle', noun, the flower cowslip) for a while, waiting for Komol to play. This is one of those where it is very easy to throw the seven-letter word down almost without thinking once it is your turn.

But that would have been a huge mistake. An improbable floater gave me an even better eight-letter play. It only actually scores one more point than **PAIGLES**, but the tactical difference is huge. I played **SLIP(P)AGE** at B4d for eighty.

(-38) <u>KOMOL 309</u>–347 CRAIG

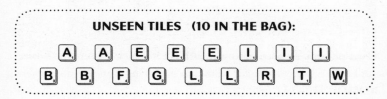

That was pretty much worse-case scenario for Komol. He has to nothing to score with and needs to make something happen, or he's going to end with a whimper. In an even game, **DOG(G)O** at H1a for twenty-four, keeping **ACK,** would be a really nice play (as well as being an interesting adjective meaning "in hiding and keeping quiet"). But it doesn't really make anything happen, and would be unlikely to force a win.

Komol spots a more creative option, playing **DOG** at M14d for seventeen. This creates a dangerous opening in column 15. With a leave of **ACKO** it's unlikely to be much use next turn; however, chances are that it will get blocked anyway, and with six letters needed to hit the triple word score, it will be hard enough to score off, but useful enough to be a big threat.

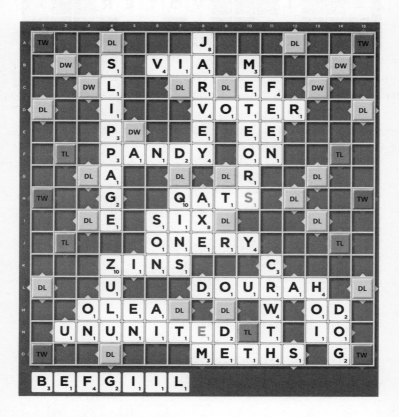

KOMOL 326–347 CRAIG (+21)

The bonus **FILIBEG** (a kilt; the word has numerous different spellings) sits on the rack, but there's nowhere on the board to put it. With the unseen tiles as they are, there are all sorts of possibilities onto the newly created opening. Unfortunately not quite as many with **BEFGIIL**. I don't think there's any real doubt that you have to play in column 15 here. It's the only significant threat.

There are a few options to choose from: **LIFE**, **BILGE**, **GIE**, to name some better ones. With seven in the bag, **BILGE** is attractive because leaving two makes it much harder to create an opening, score, and leave anything. But **BILGE** also creates a big spot for the **K**, and the lead isn't big enough to disregard it. **LIFE**'s leave is a bit clunky. **GIE** doesn't score that much. The best move is **GIBE** at J15d, netting fourteen and leaving a reasonably productive **FIL**. That's what I played.

(-35) **KOMOL 326–361 CRAIG**

UNSEEN TILES (3 IN THE BAG):

A A E I I B F L L W

A pretty nice pickup of **ERT**, and suddenly things look bonus-friendly. But can Komol realistically get a word that will fit in column 14, whilst also opening up the left side of the board? Well, If he were to just dump the **K** at G3, then an **I** pickup would mean **EROTICA** would play. But that's the only option by playing off one tile. Two out of eleven aren't great odds, and even if the bonus went down, you wouldn't be guaranteed to win.

A thirty-five point deficit is still catchable without a bonus, but it needs to threaten, and so force a defensive play or a mistake. **KA** at G3d for twenty-five does just that. With **O(KA)** and **A(KA)** possible, it creates a few headaches, and **ECORT** is a strong leave, particularly with only the **E** duplicated in the unseen tiles (so a multitude of options are pretty much guaranteed next turn). Komol piles the pressure on with **KA**.

KOMOL 351–361 CRAIG (+10)

As is often the case, I hadn't left myself a huge amount of time to figure this particular conundrum out. There are two possible bonus plays with the unseen tiles, **OCREATE**, and **COWTREE**. Fortunately, neither will fit on the right side of the board. With little scoring potential on the board, blocking the new opening and scoring reasonably well should be sufficient to clinch the game.

A(KA) and **O(KA)** are the main threats in the second column. If I play the former, I have to be wary that **AKA** in turn takes **T** and **W** hooks. Playing **BL(AG)** or **FL(AG)** at H1 seems reasonable, but then that requires working out if there are any potential bonuses going through. Indeed **CROW(F)EET** (plural of crowfoot, a plant) could play through an **F**. If you're confident and have time to work through everything, the best move is **ALIF** (first letter of the Arabic alphabet) at G2d for twenty-six. Whilst it looks so dangerous to have **LAG** next to the triple word score, there's no way for Komol to capitalize on it, and it provides a scoring spot for the **B**. But it takes a confident player to commit to **ALIF**.

The main scoring threat apart from a bonus is actually **COW(P)EA** (a tropical climbing plant) at E1a for thirty-two. So playing off one tile at I3 looks risky, but simply putting a **B** or **W** there wins every time if the endgame is played optimally. Again, it's difficult to work through those permutations. The most clear option that wins every time is **FIB** at H2d for twenty-one. Unfortunately, I went with **FLAIL** at the same spot for seventeen.

(-27) **KOMOL 351–378 CRAIG**

UNSEEN TILES:

A   I   B

If the **C** or **W** had been in the bag, then I would have had no way of scoring or going out in one, whilst Komol would simply have needed to find a good out-in-two combination. I had blocked **COWTREE** (A South American tree), but is there any way of conjuring up an unlikely win from here?

With **ABI** on my rack, there are outs with **BIA(S)** at B1a, **BAI(L)** at C1a, and the more obscure **BA(N)I** at D6d. It isn't possible to block all of them, though. Blocking the first two is simple, so the best chance is to do that and hope **BA(N)I** is missed. **WEET** (verb, to know, or adjective, wet) at A3d for twenty-two fits the bill nicely. With **ORC** to play in a couple of spots, anything but **BA(N)I** will mean a victory. Komol plays **WEET**.

KOMOL 373–378 CRAIG (+5)

UNSEEN TILES:

O₁ C₃ R₁

No mistakes this time. I put down **BA(N)I** (the plural form of a monetary unit from Romania and Moldova) to win 389–368. Komol played almost perfectly, whilst I made a number of minor errors which, fortunately for me, didn't prove costly at the end.

Komol went on to make the final, eventually losing out 3–2 to Nigel Richards, whilst I went on to finish fifth.

Study

It is surprising just how many players study. I come across a few tournament regulars here and there who boast that they've never bothered, but even at the lowest levels of competitive play, people tend to put some work in, whether they admit it or not.

Ultimately, if you have ambitions of playing at a tournament, the only thing that's really mandatory is knowing the two-letter words. Without them it will be quite a frustrating experience all round. After that it is entirely up to the individual. Some like to learn words on a particular topic (the ABSP site is well stocked with these thanks to David Sutton). A few like to study words with a particular suffix or prefix (I went through a phase of learning -**OLOGY** words). Others enjoy learning every anagram or subanagram of a loved one's name, with a requisite number of blanks thrown in.

The important thing is to learn what you want to learn and in a way that you enjoy, or at least find tolerable. It's not important to remember what each word means, but it is often quite useful to know. Personally I find it takes a lot more effort to memorize definitions. As well as developing your word knowledge, it's also helpful to build up your anagramming muscle. The obvious aspect is that it helps you find words in a game, but it also means you can cover more words in the same amount of time when you're swotting up. This can have an enormous impact if you're putting serious hours into study. Before I really studied, I'd played many years of fast online games. That meant I developed a pretty good core of words I could play without hesitation. They were second nature to me. The advantage of playing them is you will find it much easier to spot them during an actual game. It is one thing to know a word, it is another to see it, particularly if it's somewhat counterintuitive, such as **SJOE** or **WAQF**. I won't tell you how easy it is to see **JOE** on the board and forget **SJOE** exists – at least until you've played it once or twice. Another difference is that between 'knowing' a word and being ready to play it in an environment where moves can be challenged and if something's invalid a turn is lost. If you play double challenge, then it can help with the bravery of playing words, but challenging them is tougher.

So onto what I did for studying. I started off with a program called *LeXpert*, which is no longer maintained, and went through threes, fours, and a few high-probability sevens and eights. Now and then I'd go through the bonus length stuff – it was much more fun. Eventually other programs or websites popped up. One called *JumbleTime* I enjoyed, which was much better for raw anagramming power, but not so great for word security (being sure whether a word is good or not). The modern equivalents of these two are *Zyzzyva* and *Aerolith*.

Essentially, *LeXpert*, *JumbleTime*, *Zyzzyva*, and *Aerolith* all worked by giving you a scrambled set of letters which have at least one anagram in it. But the presentation was different. *JumbleTime* and *Aerolith* presented you with a wall of around fifty sets, and you had a time limit to find the answers, which were revealed at the end. The other two programs worked by giving you one bunch of letters at a time. The answers were then revealed, depending on how you had it set up.Over the past decade or so, I went through periods when I spent as much as three hours a day doing cardbox study on *Zyzzyva*. The principle of the cardbox system is if you failed to correctly answer a given set of letters, you would be quizzed on it the next day. But if you got it right and continued doing so, then you would be tested on that particular question less and less often, up to the point where eventually it would only be scheduled to come up around once a year. As well as anagrams, you can do quizzes on hooks, or both.

In theory I know every word up to eight letters long, apart from a load of sixes. But I don't expect everyone else to learn 100,000 words or so. If you want to learn words purely by their usefulness in Scrabble then start with the shortest first. Six-letter words throw things out a little bit, because they're less useful than bonus length words (sevens and eights). Breaking down those words further, you would generally prioritize vowel-heavy and consonant-heavy words next, as well as shorter **JQXZ** words.

If you're getting quite serious, then you would move on to high probability or playability words. Probability refers to the odds of simply drawing tiles out of a bag, and how likely a particular set is to come out. So **NOTAIRE/OTARINE** is the highest probability seven, because it uses all of the most common tiles in Scrabble. Playability refers to how often a computer player would actually use a given word in an almost endless number of games. This is a better measure of utility than probability.

It is important to stress the difference between a relative newbie to studying and an international player. As well as the word knowledge, an international player is capable of spotting the majority of words almost instantaneously. For instance, in *Aerolith*, where you are presented with a wall of fifty jumbled up sets, I will typically find all the seven-letter words (usually about seventy answers, as some sets have multiple anagrams) in about two minutes, and the eight-letter words (usually around sixty) in 2½ minutes. In *Zyzzyva* I go through about 700 racks an hour. With practice, anyone will get an awful lot faster and more proficient. It's almost an exponential rate of improvement, so don't be disheartened, wherever your skill level is currently at.

The other way to learn is playing. You will pick up some of the most frequent and useful words by simply having matches against others. More so against a computer, which has full word knowledge, so will put down more obscurities than a human opponent. It will also help to solidify certain words, unusual hooks, and so on. But ultimately you will only learn a fraction of the words this way. Playing will initially be important, getting used to certain things, developing experience for endgame play, and other nuanced strategy. But after that it has little benefit to improving your Scrabble. To go further, it becomes about learning words, and occasionally analyzing games on a program such as *Quackle* or *Elise*, to see what mistakes you're making, if any.

I would also caution about playing online or against the computer too much if you're competing in tournaments face-to-face. It is easy to get into bad, lazy habits. It is also significantly different actually looking at a computer screen and spotting plays than it is finding moves with a physical Scrabble set in front of you.

Words & Definitions

Introduction

You may think the longer the word is, the more useful it will be because it is likely to score more. However it isn't as simple as that.

There will be dozens of two and three letter words played in a typical game at any level, whilst even at a World Championship a player will only average two to three words of seven or eight letters long.

You then have to consider that there are over 75,000 seven and eight letter words combined, compared to 124 allowable two letter words and 1,341 three letter words. So a particular short word is that much more likely to come up because there aren't as many to choose from.

Two-letter words

Here is the first, essential thing you have to know to improve your game: All 124 of them in Collins Official Scrabble Words. See pages 180 – 184.

Three-letter words

But it doesn't end there. Three-letter words are also important for helping you build up your moves. Because there are a lot more of these than twos it will take a few months for them to become familiar. The inflexibility of the higher value tiles as well as their increased potential to score means smaller words with J, Q, X and Z are particularly important and a priority to learn. See pages 185 – 233.

Two-Letter Words (with Definitions)

AA   *noun* volcanic rock

AB   *noun* abdominal muscle

AD   *noun* advertisement

AE   *determiner* one

AG   *noun* agriculture

AH   *exclamation* expression surprise, joy; *verb* say ah

AI   *noun* shaggy-coated slow-moving animal of South America

AL   *noun* Asian shrub or tree

AM   first person singular present tense of *be*

AN   *determiner* form of *a* used before vowels; *noun* additional condition

AR   *noun* letter R

AS   *adverb* used to indicate amount or extent in comparisons; *noun* ancient Roman unit of weight

AT   *noun* Laotian monetary unit worth one hundredth of a kip

AW   variant of *all*

AX   same as *axe*

AY   *adverb* ever; *noun* expression of agreement

BA   *noun* symbol for the soul in ancient Egyptian religion

BE   *verb* exist or live

BI   short for *bisexual*

BO   *exclamation* uttered to startle or surprise someone; *noun* fellow, buddy

BY   *preposition* indicating the doer of an action, nearness, movement past, time before or during which, etc; *noun* pass to the next round (of a competition, etc)

CH   obsolete form of *I*

DA   *noun* Burmese knife

DE   *preposition* of or from

DI   plural of *deus*, god.

DO   *verb* perform or complete (a deed or action); *noun* party, celebration

EA	*noun* river
ED	*noun* education
EE	Scots word for *eye* (plural **EEN**)
EF	*noun* letter F
EH	*exclamation* of surprise or inquiry; *verb* say eh
EL	*noun* American elevated railway
EM	*noun* square of a body of any size of type, used as a unit of measurement
EN	*noun* unit of measurement, half the width of an em
ER	interjection made when hesitating in speech
ES	*noun* letter S
ET	dialect past tense of *ate*
EX	*prepositions* not including; *noun* former husband, wife, etc; *verb* cross out or delete
FA	*noun* (in tonic sol-fa) fourth degree of any major scale
FE	*noun* variant of Hebrew letter *pe*, transliterated as *f*
FY	*exclamation* of disaproval
GI	*noun* white suit worn in martial arts
GO	*verb* move to or from a place; *noun* attempt
GU	*noun* type of violin used in Shetland
HA	*exclamation* of triumph, surprise, or scorn
HE	*pronoun* male person or animal; *noun* male person or animal; expression of amusement or derision
HI	*interjection* hello
HM	sound made to express hesitation or doubt
HO	*noun* derogatory term for a woman; *interjection* imitation or representation of the sound of a deep laugh; *verb* halt
ID	*noun* mind's instinctive unconscious energies
IF	*noun* uncertainty or doubt
IN	*preposition* indicating position inside, state, or situation, etc; *adverb* indicating position inside, entry into, etc.; *adjective* fashionable; *noun* way of approaching or befriending a person; *verb* take in
IO	*exclamation* of trimph; *noun* cry of io

IS	third person singular present tense of *be*
IT	*pronoun* refers to a nonhuman, animal, plant, or inanimate object; *noun* player whose turn it is to catch the others in children's games
JA	*interjection and sentence substitute* yes
JO	*noun* Scots word for sweetheart (plural **JOES**)
KA	*noun* (in ancient Egypt) type of spirit; *verb* help
KI	*noun* vital energy
KO	*noun* (in New Zealand) traditional digging tool
KY	*plural noun* Scots word for cows
LA	*exclamation* of surprise or emphasis; *noun* the sixth note of the musical scale
LI	*noun* Chinese measurement of distance
LO	*interjection* look!
MA	*noun* mother
ME	*pronoun* refers to the speaker or writer
MI	*noun* (in tonic sol-fa) third degree of any major scale
MM	expression of enjoyment of taste or smell
MO	*noun* moment
MU	*noun* twelveth letter in the Greek alphabet
MY	*adjective* belonging to me; *interjection exclamation* of surprise or awe
NA	Scots word for *no*
NE	*conjunction* nor
NO	*interjection* expresses denial, disagreement, refusal; *adjective/adverb* not any, not a, not at all; *noun* answer or vote of no
NU	*noun* thirteenth letter in the Greek alphabet
NY	nigh
OB	*noun* expression of opposition
OD	*noun* hypothetical force
OE	*noun* grandchild
OF	*preposition* belonging to
OH	*exclamation* of surprise, pain, etc; *verb* say oh
OI	shout to attract attention; *noun* grey-faced petrel
OM	*noun* sacred syllable in Hinduism

ON	*prepositon* indicating position above, attachment, closeness, etc; *adjectivel adverb* in operation; *noun* side of the field on which the batsman stands (in cricket); *verb* go on
OO	*noun* Scots word for *wool*
OP	*noun* operation
OR	*preposition* before; *adjective* of the metal gold; *noun* gold
OS	*noun* mouth or mouthlike part or opening
OU	*interjection* expressing concession; *noun* man, bloke, or chap
OW	*exclamation* of pain
OX	*noun* castrated bull
OY	*noun* grandchild
PA	*noun* (formerly) fortified Māori settlement
PE	*noun* seventeenth letter of the Hebrew alphabet, transliterated as *p*
PI	*noun* sixteenth letter in the Greek alphabet; *verb* spill and mix (set type) indiscriminately
PO	*noun* chamber pot
QI	*noun* vital force
RE	*preposition* concerning; *noun* the second note of the musical scale
SH	*interjection* hush
SI	*noun* (in tonic sol-fa) seventh degree of any major scale
SO	*adverb* to such an extent; *exclamation* of surprise, triumph, or realization; *noun* the fifth note of the musical scale
ST	*exclamation* to attract attention
TA	*interjection* thank you
TE	*noun* (in tonic sol-fa) seventh degree of any major scale
TI	*noun* (in tonic sol-fa) seventh degree of any major scale
TO	*preposition* indicating movement towards, equality, or comparison, etc; *adverb* a closed position
UG	*verb* hate
UH	*interjection* used to express hesitation
UM	representation of a common sound made when hesitating in speech; *verb* hesitate while speaking
UN	*pronoun* spelling of *one* to reflect dialectal or informal pronunciation

UP	*adverb* indicating movement to or position at a higher place; *adjective* of a high or higher position; *verb* increase or raise
UR	hestitant utterance used to fill gaps in talking
US	*pronoun* refers to the speaker or writer and another person or other people
UT	syllable used in the fixed system of solmization for the note C
WE	*pronoun* speaker or writer and one or more others
WO	archaic spelling of *woe*
XI	*noun* fourteenth letter in the Greek alphabet
XU	*noun* Vietnamese currency unit
YA	*pronoun* you
YE	*pronoun* you; *determiner* the
YO	expression used as a greeting
YU	*noun* jade
ZA	*noun* pizza
ZO	*noun* Tibetan breed of cattle

Three-Letter Words (with Definitions)

AAH   *verb* exclaim in pleasure

AAL   *noun* Asian shrub or tree

AAS   inflected form of *aa*

ABA   *noun* type of Syrian cloth

ABB   *noun* yarn used in weaving

ABO   *noun* offensive word for an Aborigine

ABS   inflected form of *ab*

ABY   *verb* pay the penalty for

ACE   *noun* playing card with one symbol on it; *adjective* excellent; *verb* serve an ace in racquet sports

ACH   Scots expression of surprise

ACT   *noun* thing done; *verb* do something

ADD   *verb* combine (numbers or quantities)

ADO   *noun* fuss, trouble

ADS   inflected form of *ad*

ADZ   *noun* (US) woodworking tool; *verb* use an adz

AFF   same as *off*

AFT   *adjective/adverb* at or towards the rear of a ship or aircraft

AGA   *noun* title of respect

AGE   *noun* length of time a person or thing has existed; *verb* make or grow old

AGO   *adverb* in the past

AGS   inflected form of *ag*

AHA   exclamation

AHI   *noun* yellowfin tuna

AHS   inflected form of *ah*

AIA   *noun* female servant in East

AID   *noun* (give) assistance or support; *verb* help financially or in other ways

AIL   *verb* trouble, afflict

AIM   *verb* point (a weapon or missile) or direct (a blow or remark) at a target; noun aiming

AIN   *noun* sixteenth letter in the Hebrew alphabet

AIR   *noun* mixture of gases forming the earth's atmosphere; verb make known publicly

AIS   inflected form of ai

AIT   *noun* islet, esp in a river

AJI   *noun* type of spicy pepper

AKA   *noun* type of New Zealand vine

AKE   *verb* old spelling of ache

ALA   *noun* winglike structure

ALB   *noun* long white robe worn by a Christian priest

ALE   *noun* kind of beer

ALF   *noun* uncultivated Australian

ALL   *adjective* whole quantity or number (of); *adverb* wholly, entirely; noun entire being, effort, or property

ALP   *noun* high mountain

ALS   inflected form of al

ALT   *noun* octave directly above the treble staff

ALU   *noun* (in Indian cookery) potato

AMA   *noun* vessel for water

AME   *noun* soul

AMI   *noun* male friend

AMP   *noun* ampere; verb excite or become excited

AMU   *noun* unit of mass

ANA   *adverb* in equal quantities; noun collection of reminiscences

AND   *noun* additional matter or problem

ANE   Scots word for one

ANI   *noun* tropical bird

ANN   *noun* old Scots word for a widow's pension

ANS   *plural noun* as in ifs and ans things that might have happened, but which did not

ANT   *noun* small insect living in highly-organized colonies

ANY	*adjective* one or some, no matter which; *adverb* at all
APE	*noun* tailless monkey such as the chimpanzee or gorilla; *verb* imitate
APO	*noun* type of protein
APP	*noun* application program
APT	*adjective* having a specified tendency; *verb* be fitting
ARB	*noun* arbitrage: purchase of currencies, securities, or commodities in one market for immediate resale in others in order to profit from unequal prices
ARC	*noun* part of a circle or other curve; *verb* form an arc
ARD	*noun* primitive plough
ARE	*noun* unit of measure, 100 square metres; *verb* used as the singular form with you
ARF	*noun* barking sound
ARK	*noun* boat built by Noah, which survived the Flood; *verb* place in an ark
ARM	*noun* limbs from the shoulder to the wrist; *verb* supply with weapons
ARS	inflected form of ar
ART	*noun* creation of works of beauty, esp paintings or sculpture
ARY	dialect form of any
ASH	*noun* powdery substance left when something is burnt; *verb* reduce to ashes
ASK	*verb* say (something) in a form that requires an answer
ASP	*noun* small poisonous snake
ASS	*noun* donkey
ATE	past tense of eat
ATS	inflected form of at
ATT	*noun* old Siamese coin
AUA	*noun* yellow-eye mullet
AUE	Māori exclamation
AUF	old word for oaf
AUK	*noun* sea bird with short wings
AVA	*adverb* at all; *noun* Polynesian shrub

AVE *noun* expression of welcome or farewell

AVO *noun* Macao currency unit

AWA same as away

AWE *noun* wonder and respect mixed with dread; *verb* fill with awe

AWK *noun* type of programming language

AWL *noun* pointed tool for piercing wood, leather, etc

AWN *noun* bristles on grasses

AXE *noun* tool with a sharp blade for felling trees or chopping wood; *verb* dismiss (employees), restrict (expenditure), or terminate (a project)

AYE *noun* affirmative vote or voter; *adverb* always

AYS inflected form of ay

AYU *noun* small Japanese fish

AZO *adjective* of the divalent group -N:N-

BAA *verb* the characteristic bleating sound of a sheep; *noun* cry made by a sheep

BAC *noun* baccalaureate

BAD *adjective* not good; *noun* unfortunate or unpleasant events collectively; *adverb* badly

BAG *noun* flexible container with an opening at one end; *verb* put into a bag

BAH expression of contempt or disgust

BAL *noun* balmoral: laced walking shoe

BAM *verb* cheat

BAN *verb* prohibit or forbid officially; *noun* official prohibition

BAP *noun* large soft bread roll

BAR *noun* rigid usually straight length of metal, wood, etc, longer than it is wide or thick; *verb* fasten or secure with a bar

BAS inflected form of ba

BAT *noun* any of various types of club used to hit the ball in certain sports; *verb* strike with or as if with a bat

BAY *noun* wide semicircular indentation of a shoreline; *verb* howl in deep tones

BED	*noun* piece of furniture on which to sleep; *verb* plant in a bed
BEE	*noun* insect that makes wax and honey
BEG	*verb* solicit (money, food, etc), esp in the street
BEL	*noun* unit for comparing two power levels or measuring the intensity of a sound
BEN	*noun* mountain peak; *adverb* in; *adjective* inner
BES	*noun* second letter of the Hebrew alphabet, transliterated as b
BET	*noun* wager between two parties predicting different outcomes of an event; *verb* make or place a bet with (a person or persons)
BEY	*noun* (in the Ottoman empire) a title given to senior officers, provincial governors, and certain other officials
BEZ	*noun* part of deer's horn
BIB	*noun* bibcock: tap with a nozzle bent downwards
BID	*verb* offer (an amount) in attempting to buy something; *noun* offer of a specified amount, as at an auction
BIG	*adjective* of considerable size, height, number, or capacity; *adverb* on a grand scale; *verb* build
BIN	*noun* container for rubbish or for storing grain, coal, etc; *verb* put in a rubbish bin
BIO	short for biography
BIS	*adverb* twice; *sentence substitute* encore! again!
BIT	*noun* small piece, portion, or quantity
BIZ	*noun* business
BOA	*noun* large nonvenomous snake
BOB	*verb* move or cause to move up and down repeatedly; *noun* short abrupt movement, as of the head
BOD	*noun* person
BOG	*noun* wet spongy ground; *verb* mire or delay
BOH	same as bo
BOI	*noun* lesbian who dresses like a boy
BOK	*noun* S African antelope
BON	*adjective* good
BOO	shout of disapproval; *verb* shout "boo" to show disapproval

BOP *verb* dance to pop music; *noun* form of jazz with complex rhythms and harmonies

BOR *noun* neighbour

BOS inflected form of bo

BOT *noun* larva of a botfly

BOW *verb* lower (one's head) or bend (one's knee or body) as a sign of respect or shame; *noun* movement made when bowing

BOX *noun* container with a firm flat base and sides; *verb* put into a box

BOY *noun* male child; *verb* act the part of a boy in a play

BRA *noun* woman's undergarment

BRO *noun* family member

BRR interjection used to suggest shivering

BRU South African word for friend

BUB *noun* youngster

BUD *noun* swelling on a plant that develops into a leaf or flower; *verb* produce buds

BUG *noun* insect; *verb* irritate

BUM *noun* buttocks or anus; *verb* get by begging; *adjective* of poor quality

BUN *noun* small sweet bread roll or cake

BUR *noun* small rotary file; *verb* form a rough edge on (a workpiece)

BUS *noun* large motor vehicle for carrying passengers between stops; *verb* travel by bus

BUT *preposition* except; *adverb* only; *noun* outer room of a two-roomed cottage: usually the kitchen

BUY *verb* acquire by paying money for; *noun* thing acquired through payment

BYE *noun* situation where a player or team wins a round by having no opponent; interjection goodbye

BYS inflected form of by

CAA a Scot word for call

CAB *noun* taxi; *verb* take a taxi

CAD *noun* dishonourable man

CAF short for cafeteria

CAG	*noun* cagoule: lightweight hooded waterproof jacket
CAL	short for calorie
CAM	*noun* device that converts a circular motion to a to-and-fro motion; *verb* furnish (a machine) with a cam
CAN	*verb* be able to; *noun* metal container for food or liquids
CAP	*noun* soft close-fitting covering for the head; *verb* cover or top with something
CAR	*noun* motor vehicle designed to carry a small number of people
CAT	*noun* small domesticated furry mammal; *verb* flog with a cat-'o-nine-tails
CAW	*noun* cry of a crow, rook, or raven; *verb* make this cry
CAY	*noun* low island or bank composed of sand and coral fragments
CAZ	short for casual
CEE	*noun* third letter of the alphabet
CEL	short for celluloid
CEP	*noun* edible woodland fungus
CHA	*noun* tea
CHE	*pronoun* dialectal form of I
CHI	*noun* twenty-second letter of the Greek alphabet
CID	*noun* leader
CIG	same as cigarette
CIS	*adjective* having two groups of atoms on the same side of a double bond
CIT	*noun* pejorative term for a town dweller
CLY	*verb* to steal or seize
COB	*noun* stalk of an ear of maize; *verb* beat, esp on the buttocks
COD	*noun* large food fish of the North Atlantic; *adjective* having the character of an imitation or parody; *verb* make fun of
COG	*noun* one of the teeth on the rim of a gearwheel; *verb* roll (cast-steel ingots) to convert them into blooms
COL	*noun* high mountain pass
CON	*verb* deceive, swindle; *noun* convict; *preposition* with

COO   *verb* (of a dove or pigeon) make a soft murmuring sound; *noun* sound of cooing; exclamation of surprise, awe, etc

COP   same as copper

COR   exclamation of surprise, amazement, or admiration

COS   *noun* cosine: trigonometric function

COT   *noun* baby's bed with high sides; *verb* entangle or become entangled

COW   *noun* mature female of certain mammals; *verb* intimidate, subdue

COX   *noun* coxswain; *verb* act as cox of (a boat)

COY   *adjective* affectedly shy or modest; *verb* to caress

COZ   archaic word for cousin

CRU   *noun* (in France) a vineyard, group of vineyards, or wine-producing region

CRY   *verb* shed tears; *noun* fit of weeping

CUB   *noun* young wild animal such as a bear or fox; *adjective* young or inexperienced; *verb* give birth to cubs

CUD   *noun* partially digested food chewed by a ruminant

CUE   *noun* signal to an actor or musician to begin speaking or playing; *verb* give a cue to

CUM   *preposition* with; *noun* vulgar and offensive word for semen; *verb* vulgar and offensive word for ejaculate

CUP   *noun* small bowl-shaped drinking container with a handle; *verb* form (one's hands) into the shape of a cup

CUR   *noun* mongrel dog

CUT   *verb* open up, penetrate, wound, or divide with a sharp instrument

CUZ   *noun* cousin

CWM   *noun* steep-sided semicircular hollow found in mountainous areas

DAB   *verb* pat lightly; *noun* small amount of something soft or moist

DAD   *noun* father; *verb* act or treat as a father

DAE   a Scot word for do

DAG   *noun* character; *verb* cut daglocks from sheep

DAH   *noun* long sound used in combination with the short sound in the spoken representation of Morse and other telegraphic codes

DAK   *noun* system of mail delivery or passenger transport

DAL   *noun* decalitre: ten litres

DAM   *noun* barrier built across a river to create a lake; *verb* build a dam across (a river)

DAN   *noun* in judo, any of the ten black-belt grades of proficiency

DAP   *verb* engage in a type of fly fishing

DAS   inflected form of da

DAW   *noun* archaic, dialect, or poetic name for a jackdaw; *verb* old word for dawn

DAY   *noun* period of 24 hours

DEB   *noun* debutante

DEE   a Scot word fordie

DEF   *adjective* very good

DEG   *verb* water (a plant, etc)

DEI   plural of deus (god)

DEL   *noun* differential operator

DEN   *noun* home of a wild animal; *verb* live in or as if in a den

DEP   *noun* small shop where newspapers, sweets, soft drinks, etc are sold

DEV   *noun* deva: (in Hinduism and Buddhism) divine being or god

DEW   *noun* drops of water that form on the ground at night from vapour in the air; *verb* moisten with or as with dew

DEX   *noun* dextroamphetamine

DEY   *noun* title given to commanders or governors of the Janissaries of Algiers

DIB   *verb* fish by allowing the bait to bob and dip on the surface

DID   inflected form of do

DIE   *verb* cease all biological activity permanently; *noun* shaped block used to cut or form metal

DIF   *noun* (slang) difference

DIG   *verb* cut into, break up, and turn over or remove (earth), esp with a spade; *noun* digging

DIM   *adjective* badly lit; *verb* make or become dim

DIN   *noun* loud unpleasant confused noise; *verb* instil (something) into someone by constant repetition

DIP	*verb* plunge quickly or briefly into a liquid; *noun* dipping
DIS	*verb* treat (a person) with contempt
DIT	*verb* stop something happening; *noun* short sound used in the spoken representation of telegraphic codes
DIV	*noun* stupid or foolish person
DOB	*verb* as in dob in inform against or report
DOC	same as doctor
DOD	*verb* clip
DOE	*noun* female deer, hare, or rabbit
DOF	informal South African word for stupid
DOG	*noun* domesticated four-legged mammal; *verb* follow (someone) closely
DOH	*noun* in tonic sol-fa, first degree of any major scale; exclamation of annoyance when something goes wrong
DOL	*noun* unit of pain intensity, as measured by dolorimetry
DOM	*noun* title given to various monks and to certain of the canons regular
DON	*verb* put on (clothing); *noun* member of the teaching staff at a university or college
DOO	a Scot word for dove
DOP	*verb* curtsy; *noun* tot or small drink, usually alcoholic; *verb* fail to reach the required standard in (an examination, course, etc)
DOR	*noun* European dung beetle
DOS	inflected form of do
DOT	*noun* small round mark; *verb* mark with a dot
DOW	*verb* archaic word meaning to be of worth
DOY	*noun* beloved person: used esp as an endearment
DRY	*adjective* lacking moisture; *verb* make or become dry
DSO	same as zho
DUB	*verb* give (a person or place) a name or nickname; *noun* style of reggae record production
DUD	*noun* ineffectual person or thing; *adjective* bad or useless

DUE   *verb* supply with; *adjective* expected or scheduled to be present or arrive; *noun* something that is owed or required; *adverb* directly or exactly

DUG   inflected form of dig

DUH   ironic response to a question or statement

DUI   inflected form of duo

DUM   *adjective* steamed

DUN   *adjective* brownish-grey; *verb* demand payment from (a debtor); *noun* demand for payment

DUO   same as duet

DUP   *verb* open

DUX   *noun* (in Scottish and certain other schools) the top pupil in a class or school

DYE   *noun* colouring substance; *verb* colour (hair or fabric) by applying a dye

DZO   a variant spelling of zo

EAN   *verb* give birth

EAR   *noun* organ of hearing, esp the external part of it; *verb* (of cereal plants) to develop parts that contain seeds, grains, or kernels

EAS   inflected form of ea

EAT   *verb* take (food) into the mouth and swallow it

EAU   same as ea

EBB   *verb* (of tide water) flow back; *noun* flowing back of the tide

ECH   *verb* eke out

ECO   *noun* ecology activist

ECU   *noun* any of various former French gold or silver coins

EDH   *noun* character of the runic alphabet

EDS   inflected form of ed

EEK   indicating shock or fright

EEL   *noun* snakelike fish

EEN   inflected form of ee

EEW   exclamation of disgust

EFF   *verb* euphemistic substitute for a certain offensive word

EFS	inflected form of ef
EFT	*noun* dialect or archaic name for a newt; *adverb* again
EGG	*noun* object laid by birds and other creatures, containing a developing embryo; *verb* urge or incite, esp to daring or foolish acts
EGO	*noun* conscious mind of an individual
EHS	inflected form of eh
EIK	variant form of eke
EKE	*verb* increase, enlarge, or lengthen
ELD	*noun* old age
ELF	*noun* (in folklore) small mischievous fairy; *verb* entangle (esp hair)
ELK	*noun* large deer of N Europe and Asia
ELL	*noun* obsolete unit of length
ELM	*noun* tree with serrated leaves
ELS	inflected form of el
ELT	*noun* young female pig
EME	*noun* uncle
EMO	*noun* type of music
EMS	inflected form of em
EMU	*noun* large Australian flightless bird with long legs
END	*noun* furthest point or part; *verb* bring or come to a finish
ENE	variant of even
ENG	*noun* symbol used to represent a velar nasal consonant
ENS	*noun* being or existence in the most general abstract sense
EON	*noun* two or more eras
ERA	*noun* period of time considered as distinctive
ERE	*preposition* before; *verb* plough
ERF	*noun* plot of land marked off for building purposes
ERG	*noun* ergometer: instrument measuring power or force
ERK	*noun* aircraftman or naval rating
ERM	expression of hesitation
ERN	archaic variant of earn
ERR	*verb* make a mistake

ERS	*noun* type of vetch (leguminous climbing plant)
ESS	*noun* letter S
EST	*noun* treatment intended to help people towards psychological growth
ETA	*noun* seventh letter in the Greek alphabet
ETH	same as edh
EUK	*verb* itch
EVE	*noun* evening or day before some special event
EVO	informal word for evening
EWE	*noun* female sheep
EWK	*verb* itch
EWT	archaic form of newt
EXO	informal word for excellent
EYE	*noun* organ of sight; *verb* look at carefully or warily
FAA	Scot word for fall
FAB	*adjective* excellent; *noun* fabrication
FAD	*noun* short-lived fashion
FAE	Scot word for from
FAG	*noun* boring or wearisome task; *verb* become exhausted by work
FAH	*noun* (in tonic sol-fa) fourth degree of any major scale
FAN	*noun* object used to create a current of air; *verb* blow or cool with a fan
FAP	*adjective* drunk
FAR	*adverb* at, to, or from a great distance; *adjective* remote in space or time; *verb* go far
FAS	inflected form of fa
FAT	*adjective* having excess flesh on the body; *noun* extra flesh on the body
FAW	*noun* gypsy
FAX	*noun* electronic system; *verb* send (a document) by this system
FAY	*noun* fairy or sprite; *adjective* of or resembling a fay; *verb* fit or be fitted closely or tightly
FED	*noun* FBI agent

FEE	*noun* charge paid to be allowed to do something; *verb* pay a fee to
FEG	same as fig
FEH	expression of contempt or disgust
FEM	*noun* partner in a sexual or romantic relationship who adopts a traditionally feminine role
FEN	*noun* low-lying flat marshy land
FER	same as far
FES	inflected form of fe
FET	*verb* fetch
FEU	*noun* (in Scotland) type of rent
FEW	*adjective* not many; *noun* as in the few small number of people considered as a class
FEY	*adjective* whimsically strange; *verb* clean out
FEZ	*noun* brimless tasselled cap, originally from Turkey
FIB	*noun* trivial lie; *verb* tell a lie
FID	*noun* spike for separating strands of rope in splicing
FIE	same as fey
FIG	*noun* soft pear-shaped fruit; *verb* dress (up) or rig (out)
FIL	*noun* monetary unit of Bahrain, Iraq, Jordan, and Kuwait
FIN	*noun* any of the appendages of some aquatic animals; *verb* provide with fins
FIR	*noun* pyramid-shaped tree
FIT	*verb* be appropriate or suitable for; *adjective* appropriate; *noun* way in which something fits
FIX	*verb* make or become firm, stable, or secure; *noun* difficult situation
FIZ	fizz: *verb* make a hissing or bubbling noise; *noun* hissing or bubbling noise
FLU	*noun* any of various viral infections
FLY	*verb* move through the air on wings or in an aircraft; *noun* fastening at the front of trousers; *adjective* sharp and cunning
FOB	*noun* short watch chain; *verb* cheat
FOE	*noun* enemy, opponent

FOG   *noun* mass of condensed water vapour in the lower air; *verb* cover with steam

FOH   expression of disgust

FON   *verb* compel

FOO   *noun* temporary computer variable or file

FOP   *noun* man excessively concerned with fashion; *verb* act like a fop

FOR   *preposition* indicating a person intended to benefit from or receive something, span of time or distance, person or thing represented by someone, etc

FOU   *adjective* full; *noun* bushel

FOX   *noun* reddish-brown bushy-tailed animal of the dog family; *verb* perplex or deceive

FOY   *noun* loyalty

FRA   *noun* brother: a title given to an Italian monk or friar

FRO   *adverb* away; *noun* afro

FRY   *verb* cook or be cooked in fat or oil; *noun* dish of fried food

FUB   *verb* cheat

FUD   *noun* rabbit's tail

FUG   *noun* hot stale atmosphere; *verb* sit in a fug

FUM   *noun* phoenix, in Chinese mythology

FUN   *noun* enjoyment or amusement; *verb* trick

FUR   *noun* soft hair of a mammal; *verb* cover or become covered with fur

GAB   *verb* talk or chatter; *noun* mechanical device

GAD   *verb* go about in search of pleasure; *noun* carefree adventure

GAE   Scot word for go

GAG   *verb* choke or retch; *noun* cloth etc put into or tied across the mouth

GAK   *noun* (slang) cocaine

GAL   *noun* girl

GAM   *noun* school of whales; *verb* (of whales) form a school

GAN   *verb* go

GAP   *noun* break or opening

GAR   *noun* primitive freshwater bony fish

GAS	*noun* airlike substance that is not liquid or solid; *verb* poison or render unconscious with gas
GAT	*noun* pistol or revolver
GAU	*noun* district set up by the Nazi Party
GAW	*noun* as in weather gaw partial rainbow
GAY	*adjective* homosexual; *noun* homosexual
GED	*noun* (Scots) pike: large predatory freshwater fish
GEE	mild exclamation of surprise, admiration, etc; *verb* move (an animal, esp a horse) ahead
GEL	*noun* jelly-like substance; *verb* form a gel
GEM	*noun* precious stone or jewel; *verb* set or ornament with gems
GEN	*noun* information; *verb* gain information
GEO	*noun* (esp in Shetland) a small fjord or gully
GER	*noun* portable Mongolian dwelling
GET	*verb* obtain or receive
GEY	*adverb* extremely; *adjective* gallant
GHI	*noun* (in Indian cookery) clarified butter
GIB	*noun* metal wedge, pad, or thrust bearing; *verb* fasten or supply with a gib
GID	*noun* disease of sheep
GIE	Scot word for give
GIF	*noun* file held in GIF format (a compressed format for a series of pictures)
GIG	*noun* single performance by pop or jazz musicians; *verb* play a gig or gigs
GIN	*noun* spirit flavoured with juniper berries; *verb* free (cotton) of seeds with an engine; begin
GIO	same as geo
GIP	offensive same as gyp
GIS	inflected form of gi
GIT	*noun* contemptible person; *verb* dialect version of get
GJU	*noun* type of violin used in Shetland
GNU	*noun* ox-like S African antelope

GOA	*noun* Tibetan gazelle
GOB	*noun* lump of a soft substance; *verb* spit
GOD	*noun* spirit or being worshipped as having supernatural power; *verb* deify
GOE	same as go
GON	*noun* geometrical grade
GOO	*noun* sticky substance
GOR	interjection God!; *noun* seagull
GOS	inflected form of go
GOT	inflected form of get
GOV	*noun* boss
GOX	*noun* gaseous oxygen
GOY	*noun* offensive Jewish word for a non-Jew
GRR	interjection expressing anger or annoyance
GUB	*noun* offensive name for a white man; *verb* hit or defeat
GUE	same as gju
GUL	*noun* design used in oriental carpets
GUM	*noun* any of various sticky subtances; *verb* stick with gum
GUN	*noun* weapon with a tube from which missiles are fired; *verb* cause (an engine) to run at high speed
GUP	*noun* gossip
GUR	*noun* unrefined cane sugar
GUS	inflected form of gu
GUT	*noun* intestine; *verb* remove the guts from; *adjective* basic or instinctive
GUV	informal name for governor
GUY	*noun* man or boy; *verb* make fun of
GYM	*noun* gymnasium
GYP	*verb* offensive meaning to swindle, cheat, or defraud; *noun* offensive word meaning an act or instance of cheating
HAD	*verb* Scots form of hold
HAE	Scot variant of have
HAG	*noun* ugly old woman; *verb* hack

HAH	same as ha
HAJ	*noun* pilgrimage a Muslim makes to Mecca
HAM	*noun* smoked or salted meat from a pig's thigh; *verb* overact
HAN	archaic inflected form of have
HAO	*noun* monetary unit of Vietnam
HAP	*noun* luck; *verb* cover up
HAS	third person singular present tense of have
HAT	*noun* covering for the head, often with a brim; *verb* supply (a person) with a hat or put a hat on (someone)
HAW	*noun* hawthorn berry; *verb* make an inarticulate utterance
HAY	*noun* grass cut and dried as fodder; *verb* cut, dry, and store (grass, clover, etc) as fodder
HEH	exclamation of surprise or inquiry
HEM	*noun* bottom edge of a garment; *verb* provide with a hem
HEN	*noun* female domestic fowl; *verb* lose one's courage
HEP	*adjective* aware of or following the latest trends
HER	*pronoun* refers to anything personified as feminine; *adjective* belonging to her; *determiner* of, belonging to, or associated with her
HES	inflected form of he
HET	short for heterosexual; *adjective* Scot word for hot
HEW	*verb* cut with an axe
HEX	*adjective* of or relating to hexadecimal notation; *noun* evil spell; *verb* bewitch
HEY	expression of surprise or for catching attention; *verb* perform a country dance
HIC	representation of the sound of a hiccup
HID	inflected form of hide
HIE	*verb* hurry
HIM	*pronoun* refers to a male person or animal; *noun* male person
HIN	*noun* Hebrew unit of capacity
HIP	*noun* either side of the body between the pelvis and the thigh; *adjective* aware of or following the latest trends; *exclamation* used to introduce cheers

HIS	*adjective* belonging to him
HIT	*verb* strike, touch forcefully; *noun* hitting
HMM	same as hm
HOA	offensive same as ho
HOB	*noun* flat top part of a cooker; *verb* cut or form with a hob
HOC	*adjective* Latin for this
HOD	*noun* open wooden box attached to a pole; *verb* bob up and down
HOE	*noun* long-handled tool used for loosening soil or weeding; *verb* scrape or weed with a hoe
HOG	*noun* castrated male pig; *verb* take more than one's share of
HOH	offensive same as ho
HOI	same as hoy
HOM	*noun* sacred plant of the Parsees and ancient Persians
HON	short for honey
HOO	expression of joy, excitement, etc
HOP	*verb* jump on one foot; *noun* instance of hopping
HOS	offensive inflected form of ho
HOT	*adjective* having a high temperature
HOW	*adverb* in what way, by what means; *noun* the way a thing is done; sentence substitute supposed Native American greeting
HOX	*verb* hamstring
HOY	cry used to attract someone's attention; *noun* freight barge; *verb* drive animal with cry
HUB	*noun* centre of a wheel, through which the axle passes
HUE	*noun* colour, shade
HUG	*verb* clasp tightly in the arms, usually with affection; *noun* tight or fond embrace
HUH	exclamation of derision or inquiry
HUI	*noun* meeting of Māori people
HUM	*verb* make a low continuous vibrating sound; *noun* humming sound
HUN	*noun* member of any of several nomadic peoples
HUP	*verb* cry hup to get a horse to move
HUT	*noun* small house, shelter, or shed

HYE	same as hie
HYP	short for hypotenuse
ICE	*noun* water in the solid state, formed by freezing liquid water; *verb* form or cause to form ice
ICH	archaic form of eke
ICK	expression of disgust
ICY	*adjective* very cold
IDE	*noun* silver orfe fish
IDS	inflected form of id
IFF	conjunction in logic, a shortened form of if and only if
IFS	inflected form of if
IGG	*verb* antagonize
ILK	*noun* type; *determiner* each
ILL	*adjective* not in good health; *noun* evil, harm; *adverb* badly
IMP	*noun* (in folklore) creature with magical powers; *verb* method of repairing the wing of a hawk or falcon
ING	*noun* meadow near a river
INK	*noun* coloured liquid used for writing or printing; *verb* mark in ink (something already marked in pencil)
INN	*noun* pub or small hotel, esp in the country; *verb* stay at an inn
INS	inflected form of *in*
ION	*noun* electrically charged atom
IOS	inflected form of *io*
IRE	*verb* anger; *noun* anger
IRK	*verb* irritate, annoy
ISH	*noun* issue
ISM	*noun* doctrine, system, or practice
ISO	*noun* short segment of film that can be replayed easily
ITA	*noun* type of palm
ITS	*determiner* belonging to it; *adjective* of or belonging to it
IVY	*noun* evergreen climbing plant
IWI	*noun* Māori tribe
JAB	*verb* poke sharply; *noun* quick punch or poke

JAG	*noun* period of uncontrolled indulgence in an activity; *verb* cut unevenly
JAI	*interjection* victory (to)
JAK	same as *jack*
JAM	*verb* pack tightly into a place; *noun* fruit preserve; hold-up of traffic
JAP	*verb* splash
JAR	*noun* wide-mouthed container; *verb* have a disturbing or unpleasant effect
JAW	*noun* one of the bones in which the teeth are set; *verb* talk lengthily
JAY	*noun* type of bird
JEE	variant of *gee*
JET	*noun* aircraft driven by jet propulsion; *verb* fly by jet aircraft
JEU	*noun* game
JEW	*verb* obsolete offensive meaning to haggle; *noun* obsolete offensive word for a haggler
JIB	same as *jibe*
JIG	*noun* type of lively dance; *verb* dance a jig
JIN	*noun* Chinese unit of weight
JIZ	*noun* wig
JOB	*noun* occupation or paid employment; *verb* work at casual jobs
JOE	same as *jo*
JOG	*verb* run at a gentle pace, esp for exercise; *noun* slow run
JOL	*noun* party; *verb* have a good time
JOR	*noun* movement in Indian music
JOT	*verb* write briefly; *noun* very small amount
JOW	*verb* ring (a bell)
JOY	*noun* feeling of great delight or pleasure; *verb* feel joy
JUD	*noun* large block of coal
JUG	*noun* container for liquids; *verb* stew or boil (meat, esp hare) in an earthenware container
JUN	*noun* North and South Korean monetary unit
JUS	*noun* right, power, or authority
JUT	*verb* project or stick out; *noun* something that juts out

KAB	variant spelling of *cab*
KAE	*noun* dialect word for jackdaw or jay; *verb* (in archaic usage) help
KAF	*noun* letter of the Hebrew alphabet
KAI	*noun* food
KAK	*noun* offensive South African slang word for *faeces*
KAM	Shakespearean word for *crooked*
KAS	inflected form of *ka*
KAT	*noun* white-flowered evergreen shrub
KAW	variant spelling of *caw*
KAY	*noun* name of the letter K
KEA	*noun* large brownish-green parrot of NZ
KEB	*verb* Scots word meaning miscarry or reject a lamb
KED	*noun* as in *sheep ked* sheep tick
KEF	same as *kif*
KEG	*noun* small metal beer barrel; *verb* put in kegs
KEN	*verb* know; *noun* range of knowledge or perception
KEP	*verb* catch
KET	*noun* dialect word for *carrion*
KEX	*noun* any of several hollow-stemmed umbelliferous plants
KEY	*noun* device for operating a lock by moving a bolt; *adjective* of great importance; *verb* enter (text) using a keyboard
KHI	*noun* letter of the Greek alphabet
KID	*noun* child; *verb* tease or deceive (someone); *adjective* younger
KIF	*noun* type of drug
KIN	*noun* person's relatives collectively; *adjective* related by blood
KIP	*verb* sleep; *noun* sleep or slumber
KIR	*noun* drink made from dry white wine and cassis
KIS	inflected form of *ki*
KIT	*noun* outfit or equipment for a specific purpose; *verb* fit or provide
KOA	*noun* Hawaiian leguminous tree
KOB	*noun* any of several species of antelope

KOI	*noun* any of various ornamental forms of the common carp
KON	old word for *know*
KOP	*noun* prominent isolated hill or mountain in southern Africa
KOR	*noun* ancient Hebrew unit of capacity
KOS	*noun* Indian unit of distance
KOW	old variant of *cow*
KUE	*noun* name of the letter Q
KYE	*noun* Korean fundraising meeting
KYU	*noun* (in judo) one of the five student grades
LAB	*noun* laboratory
LAC	*noun* (in India) 100 000, esp referring to this sum of rupees
LAD	*noun* boy or young man
LAG	*verb* go too slowly, fall behind; *noun* delay between events
LAH	*noun* (in tonic sol-fa) sixth degree of any major scale
LAM	*verb* attack vigorously
LAP	*noun* part between the waist and knees when sitting; *verb* overtake so as to be one or more circuits ahead
LAR	*noun* boy or young man
LAS	inflected form of *la*
LAT	*noun* former coin of Latvia
LAV	short for *lavatory*
LAW	*noun* rule binding on a community; *verb* prosecute; *adjective* (in archaic usage) low
LAX	*adjective* not strict; *noun* laxative
LAY	inflected form of *lie*
LEA	*noun* meadow
LED	inflected form of *lead*
LEE	*noun* sheltered side; *verb* (Scots) lie
LEG	*noun* limb on which a person or animal walks, runs, or stands
LEI	inflected form of *leu*
LEK	*noun* bird display area; *verb* gather at lek
LEP	dialect word for *leap*

LES	offensive word for *lesbian*
LET	*noun* act of letting property; *verb* obstruct
LEU	*noun* monetary unit of Romania
LEV	*noun* monetary unit of Bulgaria
LEW	*adjective* tepid
LEX	*noun* system or body of laws
LEY	*noun* land under grass
LEZ	offensive word for *lesbian*
LIB	*noun* informal word for liberation; *verb* geld
LID	*noun* movable cover
LIE	*verb* make a false statement; *noun* falsehood
LIG	*noun* function with free entertainment and refreshments; *verb* attend such a function
LIN	*verb* cease
LIP	*noun* either of the fleshy edges of the mouth; *verb* touch with the lips
LIS	*noun* fleur-de-lis
LIT	*noun* (archaic) dye or colouring
LOB	*noun* ball struck in a high arc; *verb* strike in a high arc
LOD	*noun* type of logarithm
LOG	*noun* portion of a felled tree stripped of branches; *verb* saw logs from a tree
LOO	*noun* toilet; *verb* Scots word meaning love
LOP	*verb* cut away; *noun* part(s) lopped off
LOR	exclamation of surprise or dismay
LOS	*noun* approval
LOT	*pronoun* great number; *noun* collection of people or things; *verb* draw lots for
LOU	Scot word for *love*
LOW	*adjective* not high; *adverb* in a low position; *noun* low position; *verb* moo
LOX	*verb* load fuel tanks of spacecraft with liquid oxygen; *noun* kind of smoked salmon

LOY	*noun* narrow spade with a single footrest
LUD	*noun* lord; exclamation of dismay or surprise
LUG	*verb* carry with great effort; *noun* projection serving as a handle
LUM	*noun* chimney
LUN	*noun* sheltered spot
LUR	*noun* large bronze musical horn
LUV	*noun* love; *verb* love
LUX	*noun* unit of illumination; *verb* clean with a vacuum cleaner
LUZ	*noun* supposedly indestructible bone of the human body
LYE	*noun* caustic solution
LYM	*noun* lyam: leash
MAA	*verb* (of goats) bleat
MAC	*noun* macintosh
MAD	*adjective* mentally deranged, insane; *verb* make mad
MAE	*adjective* more
MAG	*verb* talk; *noun* talk
MAK	Scot word for *make*
MAL	*noun* illness
MAM	same as *mother*
MAN	*noun* adult male; *verb* supply with sufficient people for operation or defence
MAP	*noun* representation of the earth's surface or some part of it; *verb* make a map of
MAR	*verb* spoil or impair; *noun* disfiguring mark
MAS	inflected form of *ma*
MAT	*noun* piece of fabric used as a floor covering or to protect a surface; *verb* tangle or become tangled into a dense mass; *adjective* having a dull, lustreless, or roughened surface
MAW	*noun* animal's mouth, throat, or stomach; *verb* eat or bite
MAX	*verb* reach the full extent
MAY	*verb* used as an auxiliary to express possibility, permission, opportunity, etc

MED	*noun* doctor
MEE	*noun* Malaysian noodle dish
MEG	*noun* megabyte: 220 or 1 048 576 bytes
MEH	expression of indifference or boredom
MEL	*noun* pure form of honey
MEM	*noun* thirteenth letter in the Hebrew alphabet, transliterated as *m*
MEN	inflected form of *man*
MES	inflected form of *me*
MET	*noun* meteorology
MEU	*noun* European umbelliferous plant
MEW	*noun* cry of a cat; *verb* utter this cry
MHO	*noun* SI unit of electrical conductance
MIB	*noun* marble used in games
MIC	*noun* microphone
MID	*adjective* intermediate, middle; *noun* middle; *preposition* amid
MIG	*noun* marble used in games
MIL	*noun* unit of length equal to one thousandth of an inch
MIM	*adjective* prim, modest, or demure
MIR	*noun* peasant commune in prerevolutionary Russia
MIS	inflected form of *mi*
MIX	*verb* combine or blend into one mass; *noun* mixture
MIZ	shortened form of *misery*
MMM	*interjection* expressing agreement or enjoyment
MNA	*noun* ancient unit of weight and money, used in Asia Minor
MOA	*noun* large extinct flightless New Zealand bird
MOB	*noun* disorderly crowd; *verb* surround in a mob
MOC	*noun* moccasin: soft leather shoe
MOD	*noun* member of a group of fashionable young people, originally in the 1960s; *verb* modify (a piece of software or hardware)
MOE	*adverb* more; *noun* wry face
MOG	*verb* go away
MOI	*pronoun* (used facetiously) me

MOL	*noun* the SI unit mole
MOM	same as *mother*
MON	dialect variant of *man*
MOO	*noun* long deep cry of a cow; *verb* make this noise; *interjection* instance or imitation of this sound
MOP	*noun* long stick with twists of cotton or a sponge on the end, used for cleaning; *verb* clean or soak up with or as if with a mop
MOR	*noun* layer of acidic humus formed in cool moist areas
MOS	inflected form of *mo*
MOT	*noun* girl or young woman, esp one's girlfriend
MOU	Scots word for *mouth*
MOW	*verb* cut (grass or crops); *noun* part of a barn where hay, straw, etc, is stored
MOY	*noun* coin
MOZ	*noun* hex
MUD	*noun* wet soft earth; *verb* cover in mud
MUG	*noun* large drinking cup; *verb* attack in order to rob
MUM	*noun* mother; *verb* act in a mummer's play
MUN	*verb* maun: dialect word for *must*
MUS	inflected form of *mu*
MUT	another word for *em*
MUX	*verb* spoil
MYC	*noun* oncogene that aids the growth of tumorous cells
NAB	*verb* arrest (someone)
NAE	Scot word for *no*
NAG	*verb* scold or find fault constantly; *noun* person who nags
NAH	same as *no*
NAM	*noun* distraint
NAN	*noun* grandmother
NAP	*noun* short sleep; *verb* have a short sleep
NAS	*verb* has not
NAT	*noun* supporter of nationalism

NAV	short for *navigation*
NAW	same as *no*
NAY	*interjection* no; *noun* person who votes against a motion; *adverb* used for emphasis; *sentence substitute* no
NEB	*noun* beak of a bird or the nose of an animal; *verb* look around nosily
NED	*noun* derogatory name for an adolescent considered to be a hooligan
NEE	*adjective/preposition* indicating the maiden name of a married woman
NEF	*noun* church nave
NEG	*noun* photographic negative
NEK	*noun* mountain pass
NEP	*noun* catmint
NET	*noun* fabric of meshes of string, thread, or wire with many openings; *verb* catch (a fish or animal) in a net; *adjective* left after all deductions
NEW	*adjective* not existing before; *adverb* recently; *verb* make new
NIB	*noun* writing point of a pen; *verb* provide with a nib
NID	*verb* nest
NIE	archaic spelling of *nigh* (near)
NIL	*noun* nothing, zero
NIM	*noun* game involving removing one or more small items from several rows or piles; *verb* steal
NIP	*verb* hurry; *noun* pinch or light bite
NIS	*noun* friendly goblin
NIT	*noun* egg or larva of a louse
NIX	*sentence substitute* be careful! watch out!; *noun* rejection or refusal; *verb* veto, deny, reject, or forbid (plans, suggestions, etc)
NOB	*noun* person of wealth or social distinction
NOD	*verb* lower and raise (one's head) briefly in agreement or greeting; *noun* act of nodding
NOG	*noun* short horizontal timber member
NOH	*noun* stylized classic drama of Japan
NOM	*noun* name

NON	*adverb* not: expressing negation, refusal, or denial **NOO** *noun* type of Japanese musical drama
NOR	*preposition* and not
NOS	inflected form of *no*
NOT	*adverb* expressing negation, refusal, or denial
NOW	*adverb* at or for the present time
NOX	*noun* nitrogen oxide
NOY	*verb* harass
NTH	*adjective* of an unspecified number
NUB	*noun* point or gist (of a story etc); *verb* hang from the gallows
NUG	*noun* lump of wood sawn from a log
NUN	*noun* female member of a religious order
NUR	*noun* wooden ball
NUS	inflected form of *nu*
NUT	*noun* fruit consisting of a hard shell and a kernel; *verb* gather nuts
NYE	*noun* flock of pheasants; *verb* near
NYM	*adjective* as in *nym war* dispute about publishing material online under a pseudonym
NYS	inflected form of *ny*
OAF	*noun* stupid or clumsy person
OAK	*noun* deciduous forest tree
OAR	*noun* pole with a broad blade, used for rowing a boat; *verb* propel with oars
OAT	*noun* hard cereal grown as food
OBA	*noun* (in W Africa) a Yoruba chief or ruler
OBE	*noun* ancient Laconian village
OBI	*noun* broad sash tied in a large flat bow at the back; *verb* bewitch
OBO	*noun* ship carrying oil and ore
OBS	inflected form of *ob*
OCA	*noun* any of various South American herbaceous plants
OCH	expression of surprise, annoyance, or disagreement
ODA	*noun* room in a harem
ODD	*adjective* unusual

ODE   *noun* lyric poem, usually addressed to a particular subject

ODS   inflected form of *od*

OES   inflected form of *oe*

OFF   *preposition* away from; *adverb* away; *adjective* not operating; *noun* side of the field to which the batsman's feet point; *verb* kill

OFT   *adverb* often

OHM   *noun* unit of electrical resistance

OHO   *noun* exclamation expressing surprise, exultation, or derision

OHS   inflected form of *oh*

OIK   *noun* offensive word for a person regarded as inferior because ignorant or lower-class

OIL   *noun* viscous liquid, insoluble in water and usually flammable; *verb* lubricate (a machine) with oil

OIS   inflected form of *oi*

OKA   *noun* unit of weight used in Turkey

OKE   same as *oka*

OLD   *adjective* having lived or existed for a long time; *noun* earlier or past time

OLE   exclamation of approval or encouragement customary at bullfights; *noun* cry of olé

OLM   *noun* pale blind eel-like salamander

OMA   *noun* grandmother

OMS   inflected form of *om*

ONE   *adjective* single, lone; *noun* number or figure 1; *pronoun* any person

ONO   *noun* Hawaiian fish

ONS   inflected form of *on*

ONY   Scots word for *any*

OOF   *noun* money

OOH   exclamation of surprise, pleasure, pain, etc; *verb* say ooh

OOM   *noun* title of respect used to refer to an elderly man

OON   Scots word for *oven*

OOP   *verb* Scots word meaning *bind*

OOR   Scots form of *our*

OOS	inflected form of *oo*
OOT	Scots word for *out*
OPA	*noun* grandfather
OPE	archaic or poetic word for *open*
OPS	inflected form of *op*
OPT	*verb* show a preference, choose
ORA	inflected form of *os*
ORB	*noun* ceremonial decorated sphere; *verb* make or become circular or spherical
ORC	*noun* any of various whales, such as the killer and grampus
ORD	*noun* pointed weapon
ORE	*noun* (rock containing) a mineral which yields metal
ORF	*noun* infectious disease of sheep
ORG	*noun* organization
ORS	inflected form of *or*
ORT	*noun* fragment
OSE	*noun* long ridge of gravel, sand, etc
OUD	*noun* Arabic stringed musical instrument
OUK	Scots word for *week*
OUP	same as *oop*
OUR	*adjective* belonging to us; *determiner* of, belonging to, or associated in some way with us
OUS	inflected form of *ou*
OUT	*adjective* denoting movement or distance away from; *verb* name (a public figure) as being homosexual
OVA	plural of *ovum* (unfertilized egg cell)
OWE	*verb* be obliged to pay (a sum of money) to (a person)
OWL	*noun* night bird of prey; *verb* act like an owl
OWN	*adjective* used to emphasize possession; *pronoun* thing(s) belonging to a particular person; *verb* possess
OWT	dialect word for *anything*
OXO	*noun* as in *oxo acid* acid that contains oxygen
OXY	inflected form of *ox*

OYE	same as *oy*
OYS	inflected form of *oy*
PAC	*noun* soft shoe
PAD	*noun* piece of soft material used for protection, support, absorption of liquid, etc; *verb* protect or fill with soft material
PAH	same as *pa*
PAK	*noun* pack
PAL	*noun* friend; *verb* associate as friends
PAM	*noun* knave of clubs
PAN	*noun* wide long-handled metal container used in cooking; *verb* sift gravel from (a river) in a pan to search for gold
PAP	*noun* soft food for babies or invalids; *verb* (of the paparazzi) to follow and photograph (a famous person); *verb* feed with pap
PAR	*noun* usual or average condition; *verb* play (a golf hole) in par
PAS	*noun* dance step or movement, esp in ballet
PAT	*verb* tap lightly; *noun* gentle tap or stroke; *adjective* quick, ready, or glib
PAV	*noun* pavlova: meringue cake topped with whipped cream and fruit
PAW	*noun* animal's foot with claws and pads; *verb* scrape with the paw or hoof
PAX	*noun* peace; *interjection* signalling a desire to end hostilities
PAY	*verb* give money etc in return for goods or services; *noun* wages or salary
PEA	*noun* climbing plant with seeds growing in pods
PEC	*noun* pectoral muscle
PED	*noun* pannier
PEE	*verb* vulgar word for *urinate*; *noun* vulgar word for *urine*
PEG	*noun* pin or clip for joining, fastening, marking, etc; *verb* fasten with pegs
PEH	inflected form of *pe*
PEL	*noun* pixel
PEN	*noun* instrument for writing in ink; *verb* write or compose

PEP	*noun* high spirits, energy, or enthusiasm; *verb* liven by imbuing with new vigour
PER	*preposition* for each
PES	*noun* animal part corresponding to the foot
PET	*noun* animal kept for pleasure and companionship; *adjective* kept as a pet; *verb* treat as a pet
PEW	*noun* fixed benchlike seat in a church
PHI	*noun* twenty-first letter in the Greek alphabet
PHO	*noun* Vietnamese noodle soup
PHT	*interjection* expressing irritation or reluctance
PIA	*noun* innermost of the three membranes that cover the brain and the spinal cord
PIC	*noun* photograph or illustration
PIE	*noun* dish of meat, fruit, etc baked in pastry
PIG	*noun* animal kept and killed for pork, ham, and bacon; *verb* eat greedily
PIN	*noun* short thin piece of stiff wire with a point and head, for fastening things; *verb* fasten with a pin
PIP	*noun* small seed in a fruit; *verb* chirp
PIR	*noun* Sufi master
PIS	inflected form of *pi*
PIT	*noun* deep hole in the ground; *verb* mark with small dents or scars
PIU	*adverb* more (quickly, softly, etc)
PIX	less common spelling of *pyx*
PLU	*noun* (formerly in Canada) beaver skin used as a standard unit of value in the fur trade
PLY	*verb* work at (a job or trade); *noun* thickness of wool, fabric, etc
POA	*noun* type of grass
POD	*noun* long narrow seed case of peas, beans, etc; *verb* remove the pod from
POH	exclamation expressing contempt or disgust; *verb* reject contemptuously
POI	*noun* ball of woven flax swung rhythmically by Māori women during poi dances

POL   *noun* political campaigner

POM   *noun* offensive Australian and New Zealand word for an English person

POO   *verb* a childish word for *defecate*

POP   *verb* make or cause to make a small explosive sound; *noun* small explosive sound; *adjective* popular

POS   inflected form of *po*

POT   *noun* round deep container; *verb* plant in a pot

POW   exclamation to indicate that a collision or explosion has taken place; *noun* head or a head of hair

POX   *noun* disease in which skin pustules form; *verb* infect with pox

POZ   *adjective* positive

PRE   *preposition* before

PRO   *preposition* in favour of; *noun* professional; *adverb* in favour of a motion etc

PRY   *verb* make an impertinent or uninvited inquiry into a private matter; *noun* act of prying

PSI   *noun* twenty-third letter of the Greek alphabet

PST   *interjection* sound made to attract someone's attention

PUB   *noun* building with a bar licensed to sell alcoholic drinks; *verb* visit a pub or pubs

PUD   short for *pudding*

PUG   *noun* small snub-nosed dog; *verb* mix or knead (clay) with water to form a malleable mass or paste

PUH   exclamation expressing contempt or disgust

PUL   *noun* Afghan monetary unit

PUN   *noun* use of words to exploit double meanings for humorous effect; *verb* make puns

PUP   *noun* young of certain animals, such as dogs and seals; *verb* (of dogs, seals, etc) to give birth to pups

PUR   same as *purr*

PUS   *noun* yellowish matter produced by infected tissue

PUT   *verb* cause to be (in a position, state, or place); *noun* throw in putting the shot

PUY	*noun* small volcanic cone	
PWN	*verb* defeat (an opponent) in conclusive and humiliating fashion	
PYA	*noun* monetary unit of Myanmar worth one hundredth of a kyat	
PYE	same as *pie*	
PYX	*noun* any receptacle for the Eucharistic Host; *verb* put (something) in a pyx	
QAT	variant spelling of *kat*	
QIN	*noun* Chinese stringed instrument related to the zither	
QIS	inflected form of *qi*	
QUA	*preposition* in the capacity of	
RAD	*noun* former unit of absorbed ionizing radiation dose; *verb* fear; *adjective* slang term for great	
RAG	*noun* fragment of cloth; *verb* tease; *adjective* (in British universities and colleges) of various events organized to raise money for charity	
RAH	informal US word for *cheer*	
RAI	*noun* type of Algerian popular music	
RAJ	*noun* (in India) government	
RAM	*noun* male sheep; *verb* strike against with force	
RAN	inflected form of *run*	
RAP	*verb* hit with a sharp quick blow; *noun* quick sharp blow	
RAS	*noun* headland	
RAT	*noun* small rodent; *verb* inform (on)	
RAV	*noun* Hebrew word for *rabbi*	
RAW	*noun* as in *in the raw* without clothes; *adjective* uncooked	
RAX	*verb* stretch or extend; *noun* act of stretching or straining	
RAY	*noun* single line or narrow beam of light; *verb* (of an object) to emit (light) in rays or (of light) to issue in the form of rays	
REB	*noun* Confederate soldier in the American Civil War	
REC	short for *recreation*	
RED	*adjective* of a colour varying from crimson to orange and seen in blood, fire, etc; *noun* red colour	
REE	*noun* Scots word meaning a walled enclosure	

REF	*noun* referee in sport; *verb* referee
REG	*noun* large expanse of stony desert terrain
REH	*noun* (in India) salty surface crust on the soil
REI	*noun* name for a former Portuguese coin
REM	*noun* dose of ionizing radiation
REN	archaic variant of *run*
REO	*noun* New Zealand language
REP	*noun* sales representative; *verb* work as a representative
RES	informal word for *residence*
RET	*verb* moisten or soak (flax, hemp, jute, etc) to facilitate separation of fibres
REV	*noun* revolution (of an engine); *verb* increase the speed of revolution of (an engine)
REW	archaic spelling of *rue*
REX	*noun* king
REZ	*noun* informal word for an instance of reserving; reservation
RHO	*noun* seventeenth letter in the Greek alphabet
RHY	archaic spelling of *rye*
RIA	*noun* long narrow inlet of the seacoast
RIB	*noun* one of the curved bones forming the framework of the upper part of the body; *verb* provide or mark with ribs
RID	*verb* clear or relieve (of)
RIF	*verb* lay off
RIG	*verb* arrange in a dishonest way; *noun* apparatus for drilling for oil and gas
RIM	*noun* edge or border; *verb* put a rim on (a pot, cup, wheel, etc)
RIN	Scots variant of *run*
RIP	*verb* tear violently; *noun* split or tear
RIT	*verb* Scots word meaning to cut or slit
RIZ	(in some dialects) past form of *rise*
ROB	*verb* steal from
ROC	*noun* monstrous bird of Arabian mythology
ROD	*noun* slender straight bar, stick; *verb* clear with a rod

ROE   *noun* mass of eggs in a fish, sometimes eaten as food

ROK   same as *roc*

ROM   *noun* male gypsy

ROO   *noun* kangaroo

ROT   *verb* decompose or decay; *noun* decay

ROW   *noun* straight line of people or things; *verb* propel (a boat) by oars

RUB   *verb* apply pressure with a circular or backwards-and-forwards movement; *noun* act of rubbing

RUC   same as *roc*

RUD   *noun* red or redness; *verb* redden

RUE   *verb* feel regret for; *noun* plant with evergreen bitter leaves

RUG   *noun* small carpet; *verb* (in dialect) tug

RUM   *noun* alcoholic drink distilled from sugar cane; *adjective* odd, strange

RUN   *verb* move with a more rapid gait than walking; *noun* act or spell of running

RUT   *noun* furrow made by wheels; *verb* be in a period of sexual excitability

RYA   *noun* type of rug originating in Scandinavia

RYE   *noun* kind of grain used for fodder and bread

RYU   *noun* school of Japanese martial arts

SAB   *noun* person engaged in direct action to prevent a targeted activity taking place; *verb* take part in such action

SAC   *noun* pouchlike structure in an animal or plant

SAD   *adjective* sorrowful, unhappy; *verb* New Zealand word meaning to express sadness or displeasure strongly

SAE   Scot word for *so*

SAG   *verb* sink in the middle; *noun* droop

SAI   *noun* South American monkey

SAL   pharmacological term for *salt*

SAM   *verb* collect

SAN   *noun* sanatorium

SAP   *noun* moisture that circulates in plants; *verb* undermine

SAR   *noun* marine fish; *verb* Scots word meaning to savour

SAT	inflected form of *sit*
SAU	archaic past tense of *see*
SAV	*noun* saveloy: spicy smoked sausage
SAW	*noun* hand tool for cutting wood and metal; *verb* cut with a saw
SAX	same as *saxophone*
SAY	*verb* speak or utter; *noun* right or chance to speak
SAZ	*noun* Middle Eastern stringed instrument
SEA	*noun* mass of salt water covering three quarters of the earth's surface
SEC	*noun* secant: (in trigonometry) the ratio of the length of the hypotenuse to the length of the adjacent side
SED	old spelling of *said*
SEE	*verb* perceive with the eyes or mind; *noun* diocese of a bishop
SEG	*noun* metal stud on shoe sole
SEI	*noun* type of rorqual
SEL	Scot word for *self*
SEN	*noun* monetary unit of Brunei, Cambodia, Indonesia, Malaysia, and formerly of Japan
SER	*noun* unit of weight used in India
SET	*verb* put in a specified position or state; *noun* setting or being set; *adjective* fixed or established beforehand
SEV	*noun* Indian snack of deep-fried noodles
SEW	*verb* join with thread repeatedly passed through with a needle
SEX	*noun* state of being male or female; *verb* find out the sex of; *adjective* of sexual matters
SEY	*noun* Scots word meaning part of cow carcase
SEZ	*verb* informal spelling of *says*
SHA	*interjection* be quiet
SHE	*pronoun* female person or animal previously mentioned; *noun* female person or animal
SHH	*interjection* sound made to ask for silence
SHO	*adjective* sure, as pronounced in southern US
SHY	*adjective* not at ease in company; *verb* start back in fear; *noun* throw
SIB	*noun* blood relative

SIC	*adverb* thus; *verb* attack
SIF	*adjective* (South African slang) disgusting
SIG	short for *signature*
SIK	*adjective* excellent
SIM	*noun* computer game that simulates an activity
SIN	*noun* offence or transgression; *verb* commit a sin
SIP	*verb* drink in small mouthfuls; *noun* amount sipped
SIR	*noun* polite term of address for a man; *verb* call someone "sir"
SIS	*noun* sister
SIT	*verb* rest one's body upright on the buttocks
SIX	*noun* one more than five
SKA	*noun* type of West Indian pop music of the 1960s
SKI	*noun* one of a pair of long runners fastened to boots for gliding over snow or water; *verb* travel on skis
SKY	*noun* upper atmosphere as seen from the earth; *verb* hit high in the air
SLY	*adjective* crafty
SMA	Scots word for *small*
SNY	*noun* side channel of a river
SOB	*verb* weep with convulsive gasps; *noun* act or sound of sobbing
SOC	*noun* feudal right to hold court
SOD	*noun* (piece of) turf; *verb* cover with sods
SOG	*verb* soak
SOH	*noun* (in tonic sol-fa) fifth degree of any major scale
SOL	*noun* liquid colloidal solution
SOM	*noun* currency of Kyrgyzstan and Uzbekistan
SON	*noun* male offspring
SOP	*noun* concession to pacify someone; *verb* mop up or absorb (liquid)
SOS	inflected form of *so*
SOT	*noun* habitual drunkard; *adverb* indeed: used to contradict a negative statement; *verb* be a drunkard
SOU	*noun* former French coin
SOV	shortening of *sovereign*

SOW	*verb* scatter or plant (seed) in or on (the ground); *noun* female adult pig
SOX	informal spelling of *socks*
SOY	*noun* as in *soy sauce* salty dark brown sauce made from soya beans
SOZ	*interjection* (slang) sorry
SPA	*noun* resort with a mineral-water spring; *verb* visit a spa
SPY	*noun* person employed to obtain secret information; *verb* act as a spy
SRI	*noun* title of respect used when addressing a Hindu
STY	*verb* climb
SUB	*noun* subeditor; *verb* act as a substitute
SUD	singular of *suds*
SUE	*verb* start legal proceedings against
SUG	*verb* sell a product while pretending to conduct market research
SUI	*adjective* of itself
SUK	*noun* souk: open-air marketplace
SUM	*noun* result of addition, total; *verb* add or form a total of (something)
SUN	*noun* star around which the earth and other planets revolve; *verb* expose (oneself) to the sun's rays
SUP	*verb* have supper
SUQ	same as *suk*
SUR	*preposition* above
SUS	suss: *verb* attempt to work out (a situation, etc), using one's intuition; *noun* sharpness of mind
SWY	*noun* Australian gambling game involving two coins
SYE	*verb* strain
SYN	Scots word for *since*
TAB	*noun* small flap or projecting label; *verb* supply with a tab
TAD	*noun* small bit or piece
TAE	*preposition* Scots form of *to*; *verb* Scots form of *toe*
TAG	*noun* label bearing information; *verb* attach a tag to
TAI	*noun* type of sea bream
TAJ	*noun* tall conical cap worn as a mark of distinction by Muslims

TAK	Scots variant spelling of *take*
TAM	*noun* type of hat
TAN	*noun* brown coloration of the skin from exposure to sunlight; *verb* (of skin) go brown from exposure to sunlight; *adjective* yellowish-brown
TAO	*noun* (in Confucian philosophy) the correct course of action
TAP	*verb* knock lightly and usually repeatedly; *noun* light knock
TAR	*noun* thick black liquid distilled from coal etc; *verb* coat with tar
TAS	tass: *noun* cup, goblet, or glass
TAT	*noun* tatty or tasteless article(s); *verb* make a type of lace by looping a thread with a hand shuttle
TAU	*noun* nineteenth letter in the Greek alphabet
TAV	*noun* twenty-third and last letter in the Hebrew alphabet
TAW	*verb* convert skins into leather
TAX	*noun* compulsory payment levied by a government on income, property, etc to raise revenue; *verb* levy a tax on
TAY	Irish dialect word for *tea*
TEA	*noun* drink made from infusing the dried leaves of an Asian bush in boiling water; *verb* take tea
TEC	short for *detective*
TED	*verb* shake out (hay), so as to dry it
TEE	*noun* small peg from which a golf ball can be played at the start of each hole; *verb* position (the ball) ready for striking, on or as if on a tee
TEF	*noun* annual grass, of NE Africa, grown for its grain
TEG	*noun* two-year-old sheep
TEL	same as *tell*
TEN	*noun* one more than nine; *adjective* amounting to ten
TES	inflected form of *te*
TET	*noun* ninth letter of the Hebrew alphabet
TEW	*verb* work hard
TEX	*noun* unit of weight used to measure yarn density
THE	*determiner* definite article, used before a noun

THO	short for *though*
THY	*adjective* of or associated with you (thou); *determiner* belonging to or associated in some way with you (thou)
TIC	*noun* spasmodic muscular twitch
TID	*noun* girl
TIE	*verb* fasten or be fastened with string, rope, etc; *noun* long narrow piece of material worn knotted round the neck
TIG	*noun* child's game
TIK	*noun* (South African slang) crystal meth
TIL	another name for *sesame*
TIN	*noun* soft metallic element; *verb* put (food) into tins
TIP	*noun* narrow or pointed end of anything; *verb* put a tip on
TIS	inflected form of *ti*
TIT	*noun* any of various small songbirds; *verb* jerk or tug
TIX	*plural noun* tickets
TIZ	*noun* state of confusion
TOC	*noun* in communications code, signal for letter T
TOD	*noun* unit of weight, used for wool, etc; *verb* produce a tod
TOE	*noun* digit of the foot; *verb* touch or kick with the toe
TOG	*noun* unit for measuring the insulating power of duvets; *verb* dress oneself
TOM	*noun* male cat; *adjective* (of an animal) male; *verb* (offensive) prostitute oneself
TON	*noun* unit of weight
TOO	*adverb* also, as well
TOP	*noun* highest point or part; *adjective* at or of the top; *verb* form a top on
TOR	*noun* high rocky hill
TOT	*noun* small child; *verb* total
TOW	*verb* drag, esp by means of a rope; *noun* towing
TOY	*noun* something designed to be played with; *adjective* designed to be played with; *verb* play, fiddle, or flirt
TRY	*verb* make an effort or attempt; *noun* attempt or effort

TSK	*verb* utter the sound "tsk", usually in disapproval
TUB	*noun* open, usually round container; *verb* wash (oneself or another) in a tub
TUG	*verb* pull hard; *noun* hard pull
TUI	*noun* New Zealand honeyeater that mimics human speech and the songs of other birds
TUM	informal or childish word for *stomach*
TUN	*noun* large beer cask; *verb* put into or keep in tuns
TUP	*noun* male sheep; *verb* cause (a ram) to mate with a ewe
TUT	exclamation of mild disapproval, or surprise; *verb* express disapproval by the exclamation of "tut-tut"; *noun* payment system based on measurable work done
TUX	*noun* tuxedo: dinner jacket
TWA	Scots word for *two*
TWO	*noun* one more than one
TWP	*adjective* stupid
TYE	*noun* trough used in mining to separate valuable material from dross; *verb* (in mining) isolate valuable material from dross using a tye
TYG	*noun* mug with two handles
UDO	*noun* stout perennial plant of Japan and China
UDS	*interjection* God's or God save
UEY	*noun* u-turn
UFO	*noun* flying saucer
UGH	exclamation of disgust; *noun* sound made to indicate disgust
UGS	inflected form of *ug*
UKE	short form of *ukulele*
ULE	*noun* rubber tree
ULU	*noun* type of knife
UMM	same as *um*
UMP	umpire: *noun* official who rules on the playing of a game; *verb* act as umpire in (a game)
UMS	inflected form of *um*

UMU	*noun* type of oven
UNI	*noun* (in informal English) university
UNS	inflected form of *un*
UPO	*preposition* upon
UPS	inflected form of *up*
URB	*noun* urban area
URD	*noun* type of plant with edible seeds
URE	*noun* recently extinct European wild ox
URN	*noun* vase used as a container for the ashes of the dead; *verb* put in an urn
URP	dialect word for *vomit*
USE	*verb* put into service or action; *noun* using or being used
UTA	*noun* side-blotched lizard
UTE	same as *utility*
UTS	inflected form of *ut*
UTU	*noun* reward
UVA	*noun* grape or fruit resembling this
VAC	*verb* clean with a vacuum cleaner
VAE	same as *voe*
VAG	*noun* vagrant
VAN	*noun* motor vehicle for transporting goods; *verb* send in a van
VAR	*noun* unit of reactive power of an alternating current
VAS	*noun* vessel or tube that carries a fluid
VAT	*noun* large container for liquids; *verb* place, store, or treat in a vat
VAU	same as *vav*
VAV	*noun* sixth letter of the Hebrew alphabet
VAW	*noun* Hebrew letter
VEE	*noun* letter V
VEG	*noun* vegetable or vegetables; *verb* relax
VET	*verb* check the suitability of; *noun* military veteran
VEX	*verb* frustrate, annoy

VIA	*preposition* by way of; *noun* road
VID	same as *video*
VIE	*verb* compete (with someone)
VIG	*noun* interest on a loan that is paid to a moneylender
VIM	*noun* force, energy
VIN	*noun* French wine
VIS	*noun* power, force, or strength
VLY	*noun* area of low marshy ground
VOE	*noun* (in Orkney and Shetland) a small bay or narrow creek
VOG	*noun* air pollution caused by volcanic dust
VOL	*noun* heraldic wings
VOM	*verb* vomit
VOR	*verb* (in dialect) warn
VOW	*noun* solemn and binding promise; *verb* promise solemnly
VOX	*noun* voice or sound
VUG	*noun* small cavity in a rock or vein, usually lined with crystals
VUM	*verb* swear
WAB	*noun* web
WAD	*noun* black earthy ore of manganese; *noun* small mass of soft material; *verb* form (something) into a wad
WAE	old form of *woe*
WAG	*verb* move rapidly from side to side; *noun* wagging movement
WAI	*noun* (in New Zealand) water
WAN	*adjective* pale and sickly looking; *verb* make or become wan
WAP	*verb* strike
WAR	*noun* fighting between nations; *adjective* of, like, or caused by war; *verb* conduct a war
WAS	past tense of *be*
WAT	*adjective* wet; drunken
WAW	another name for *vav*
WAX	*noun* solid shiny fatty or oily substance used for sealing, making candles, etc; *verb* coat or polish with wax
WAY	*noun* manner or method; *verb* travel

WAZ   *verb* urinate; *noun* act of urinating

WEB   *noun* net spun by a spider; *verb* cover with or as if with a web

WED   *verb* marry

WEE   *adjective* small or short; *noun* instance of urinating; *verb* urinate

WEM   *noun* belly, abdomen, or womb

WEN   *noun* cyst on the scalp

WET   *adjective* covered or soaked with water or another liquid; *noun* moisture or rain; *verb* make wet

WEX   obsolete form of *wax*

WEY   *noun* measurement of weight

WHA   Scots word for *who*

WHO   *pronoun* which person

WHY   *adverb* for what reason; *pronoun* because of which; *noun* reason, purpose, or cause of something

WIG   *noun* artificial head of hair; *verb* furnish with a wig

WIN   *verb* come first in (a competition, fight, etc); *noun* victory, esp in a game

WIS   *verb* know or suppose (something)

WIT   *verb* detect; *noun* ability to use words or ideas in a clever and amusing way

WIZ   shortened form of *wizard*

WOE   *noun* grief

WOF   *noun* fool

WOG   *noun* offensive and derogatory word for a foreigner, esp one who is not White

WOK   *noun* bowl-shaped Chinese cooking pan, used for stir-frying

WON   *noun* standard monetary unit of North Korea; *verb* live or dwell

WOO   *verb* seek the love or affection of (a woman)

WOP   *verb* strike, beat, or thrash; *noun* heavy blow or the sound made by such a blow

WOS   inflected form of *wo*

WOT   past tense of *wit*

WOW	exclamation of astonishment; *noun* astonishing person or thing; *verb* be a great success with
WOX	past tense of *wax*
WRY	*adjective* drily humorous; *verb* twist or contort
WUD	Scots form of *wood*
WUS	*noun* casual term of address
WUZ	*verb* nonstandard spelling of *was*
WYE	*noun* y-shaped pipe
WYN	*noun* rune equivalent to English w
XED	*verb* marked a cross against
XIS	inflected form of *xi*
YAD	*noun* hand-held pointer used for reading the sefer torah
YAE	same as *ae*
YAG	*noun* artificial crystal
YAH	exclamation of derision or disgust; *noun* affected upper-class person
YAK	*noun* Tibetan ox with long shaggy hair; *verb* talk continuously about unimportant matters
YAM	*noun* tropical root vegetable
YAP	*verb* bark with a high-pitched sound; *noun* high-pitched bark
YAR	*adjective* nimble
YAS	inflected form of *ya*
YAW	*verb* (of an aircraft or ship) turn to one side or from side to side while moving; *noun* act or movement of yawing
YAY	*noun* cry of approval
YEA	*interjection* yes; *adverb* indeed or truly; *sentence substitute* aye; *noun* cry of agreement
YEH	*noun* positive affirmation
YEN	*noun* monetary unit of Japan; *verb* have a longing
YEP	*noun* affirmative statement
YER	*adjective* (colloquial) your; you
YES	*interjection* expresses consent, agreement, or approval; *noun* answer or vote of yes, used to express acknowledgment, affirmation, consent, etc; *verb* reply in the affirmative

YET	*adverb* up until then or now
YEW	*noun* evergreen tree with needle-like leaves and red berries
YEX	*verb* hiccup
YEZ	*interjection* yes
YGO	archaic past participle of *go*
YID	*noun* offensive word for a Jew
YIN	Scots word for *one*
YIP	*noun* emit a high-pitched bark
YOB	*noun* bad-mannered aggressive youth
YOD	*noun* tenth letter in the Hebrew alphabet
YOK	*verb* chuckle
YOM	*noun* day
YON	*adjective* that or those over there; *adverb* yonder *pronoun* that person or thing
YOU	*pronoun* person or people addressed; *noun* personality of the person being addressed
YOW	*verb* howl
YUG	*noun* (in Hindu cosmology) one of the four ages of mankind
YUK	exclamation indicating contempt, dislike, or disgust; *verb* chuckle
YUM	expression of delight
YUP	*noun* informal affirmative statement
YUS	inflected form of *yu*
ZAG	*verb* change direction sharply
ZAP	*verb* kill (by shooting); *noun* energy, vigour, or pep; exclamation used to express sudden or swift action
ZAS	inflected form of *za*
ZAX	*noun* tool for cutting roofing slate
ZEA	*noun* corn silk
ZED	*noun* British and New Zealand spoken form of the letter Z
ZEE	the US word for *zed*
ZEK	*noun* Soviet prisoner
ZEL	*noun* Turkish cymbal
ZEP	*noun* type of long sandwich

ZEX   *noun* tool for cutting roofing slate

ZHO   same as *zo*

ZIG   same as *zag*

ZIN   *noun* zinfandel: type of Californian wine

ZIP   same as *zipper*

ZIT   *noun* spot or pimple

ZIZ   *noun* short sleep; *verb* take a short sleep, snooze

ZOA   plural of *zoon* (independent animal body)

ZOL   *noun* (South African slang) a cannabis cigarette

ZOO   *noun* place where live animals are kept for show

ZOS   inflected form of *zo*

ZUZ   *noun* ancient Hebrew silver coin

ZZZ   *noun* informal word for *sleep*

Resources

ABSP (Association of British Scrabble Players) – *www.absp.org.uk*. Lots of interesting stuff on here, even if you're not based in the UK. Plenty of club and tourney info too.

AEROLITH – *aerolith.org* A web app which provides a fun and fast-paced way to learn words quickly. Excellent for anagramming practice.

CROSS-TABLES.COM LEAVE EVALUATOR – *www.cross-tables.com/leaves.php*.

COLLINS OFFICIAL SCRABBLE™ WORDS – The official wordlist endorsed by WESPA for use in Tournament & Club play worldwide, excluding USA and Canada, from 1st September 2015 and endorsed by Mattel.

ELISE – *www.codehappy.net/elise/*. Like *Quackle* (see below), capable of playing or analysing Scrabble moves.

FACEBOOK SCRABBLE – *apps.facebook.com/livescrabble/*

FACEBOOK SCRABBLE LEAGUE (FSL) – *scrabblescores.com/scrabble/*. If you play on Facebook Scrabble and fancy something a bit more structured and competitive then this site provides all that for you.

MIND SPORTS ACADEMY – *www.mindsportsacademy.com*. The Academy offers many training resources, including videos, games, puzzles and expert blogs and top tips. As well as the capacity to join an online community and play tournaments for fun and prizes.

QUACKLE – *people.csail.mit.edu/jasonkb/quackle/*.
Quackle with *Collins Official Scrabble Words 2015* (CSW 2015) is available from *www.collinsdictionary.com/word-games/scrabble-tools/*

SCRABBLE SNIPPETZ (Facebook group) – *www.wespa.org/snippetz.html*. A busy, friendly, and popular online community for Scrabble.

THE SCRABBLE PLAYER'S HANDBOOK – *www.scrabbleplayershandbook. com*. Free and very comprehensive ebook aimed at all aspiring Scrabblers, with contributions from around a dozen top players.

WESPA (the World English-Language Scrabble Players Association) – *www.wespa.org*. The global body which represents the national associations, as well as players more generally. This is the best place to visit if you can't find details on your local national association. It also has world rankings, news, and the international tournament calendar.

ZYZZYVA – *zyzzyva.net*. Word study tool used by almost every tournament player. It can also be used to find or verify words, for instance if you were sure you had a bonus but couldn't find one. Well, you can use Zyzzyva to find out. A version for use with CSW 2015, Collins Zyzzyva is available at HYPERLINK "http://www.collinsdictionary.com/word-games/scrabble-tools/" www.collinsdictionary.com/word-games/scrabble-tools/

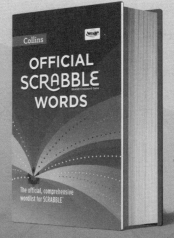